When I Rise, I Thrive

I Thrive

Healing Trauma Through Shared Stories Of Personal Transformation

Compiled By Kyra Schaefer

When I Rise, I Thrive

As You Wish Publishing, LLC
Kyra@asyouwishpublishing.com 602-592-1141

ISBN-13: 978-1-7324982-1-1

ISBN-10: 1-7324982-1-0

Library of Congress Control Number: 2019900545

Compiled by Kyra Schaefer

Edited by Todd Schaefer

Printed in the United States of America.

Nothing in this book or any affiliations with this book is a substitute for medical or psychological help. If you are needing help please seek it.

National Suicide Prevention Lifeline: 1-800-273-8255

Dedication

To the writers of the world who have begun to believe that
their story matters.

"In the darkness the tender seed believes the sun is there,
even before the ray's first kiss."

Kyra Schaefer

The winner of our Rising Star Award is Stefanie Winzer for
her article titled *Edge Of The Plane.*

Table of Contents

Introduction

The stories in this book aren't fluffy. These are real stories from real people who have come through the fires of transmutation and are able to fully embrace their healing. Our authors have come through depression, illness, abuse, accidents, divorce and issues relating to suicide. In this book, we share with you deep vulnerability, unapologetic honesty and insights about our darkest times. We are misfits, pioneers, coaches, believers, healers, and achievers who have come to understand that our deepest wounds are our greatest assets. We have come through these difficulties with forgiveness, truth, love, and wisdom. We use our stories as a way to offer hope to others in similar situations.

Are We Healed Yet?

Some stories in this book are complete, some stories of healing have just begun. But we have all learned we are in process. Healing past traumas and tragedies helps us more easily move through them, and understand the difficulties ahead. Healing one challenge doesn't mean all challenges cease to be. We know to shift our focus to allow the goodness to come to us. To let others rely on us as we rely on them, we seem to understand in the end we are all one. Gathering courage to face a new day is all we can do. We know the goodness of abiding love is all around, and accessing that love, although challenging at times, is absolutely possible.

If you are going through something right now, please know you are never alone. You may see yourself in some of these stories. Many of the authors in this book asked for help at some point in their experience; they received healing, and as a result, became healers, practitioners and coaches themselves to help others. You can find our authors' contact information in the Authors Bio Section of this book. Feel free to contact them if you need support on your journey. You don't have to do this alone. We hope these stories will help guide you, help you feel like you belong and that you will overcome any challenge, maybe not with grace or ease, but you will come through it. It's time to believe. Read on, if you dare, to unlock the possibility that everything is leading you to a greater experience of life.

Edge of the Plane
By Stefanie Winzer

I'm afraid of heights; actually, it's the falling part. I don't like small places, crowds, and strangers being too close to me. I took all of those issues and decided to package them into one activity neatly—skydiving!

My friend, Amy, gifted me a tandem jump and off we went to Eloy, Arizona. We arrived on a sunny Saturday morning with our friends and my daughters. I was pretty nervous, but tried to keep calm and stay in an active meditative state. Weeks before the jump, every time I was feeling afraid, I would picture myself at the edge of the plane. The sounds, the rushing air, the view, and the instructor saying, "One, two, three—go!" As we waited, I just kept imagining what it would be like, so I wouldn't panic and make a fool of myself.

Finally, the time came. My new best friend, Wes (my jump instructor), takes me into the prep room. First, he gives me a jumpsuit; something to cover me. Next, he tells me when we get to the edge of the plane; I have to kneel on one knee, place my hand on the straps across the chest, and lift my head. Where will my best friend Wes be? He'll be behind me. Out of my sight but with me all the way. Once we are out of the plane, I must open my arms wide, leading with my heart. If, at any time, I move my arms back in, my best friend Wes will tap me, reminding me to keep my arms and heart open. Then, he casually mentions that I may feel like I can't breathe, but that will be fear playing tricks on me. All I have to do is take a breath. Even if I'm screaming, I can still breathe. When it is time to land, my best friend Wes is in control. If I try to do it, we'll get tangled and hurt.

Before I know it, we are ascending to 13,000 feet in the crowded plane with twelve strangers. As we reach the appropriate height, my best friend Wes began to hook us together. You're probably wondering why I keep calling Wes "my best friend." I was about to strap myself to this man, putting my future and my children's future in his hands. It only seems fitting that we should be best friends. He hooked us together, my back to his front. He leads us to the edge of the plane. I kneeled, placed my hands on my heart, raised my head to the heavens and allow him to lead me out into the unknown.

With the count of three, we were in the air. At 120 mph, 13,000 feet up, my arms are open, leading with my heart, head up, and Wes at my back. I felt a tap when I need to adjust. I remembered to breathe when I felt like I couldn't.

When the pressure of falling was too much, Wes pulled the chute. Then there was stillness, beauty, and bliss. We went from falling to floating, from chaos to peace. Wes let me guide us, but he never let go of the secondary handles— ensuring that he could get us back on track if something went wrong. Then he brought us in safely for a landing.

What did I learn at the edge of the plane? Before I leap, listen to the higher voice, kneel, bring my hands to heart center, raise my head to the heavens, and lead with my heart.

Restored Dreams
By Rachel Gill

W hen I was a young girl, I was wild, energetic, and ready to plunge my heart and soul into adventures. I ran wild and barefoot along the railroad, plucking dandelions from fields, making as many wishes as I could before they fluttered to the ground. I pretended the red barn was my castle, and the hay on the ground was spun into magical gold. Every night, I would climb up onto my window seat, wish upon the stars, and clutch my favorite fairy tale book in my arms. I would pretend I was the princess in the "Happily Ever After" book. Each star twinkling in the sky held a promise of a wish to my little girl heart.

I spent my young years daydreaming under the gentle, but giant pine tree next to our house in Washington. It was my safe place. Sometimes, though, I would ride into the wind, rainbow streamers on my lavender bike, singing at the top of my lungs. I loved pretending I was Mary Poppins. I enjoyed that she could snap her fingers and make what she said become real. I wanted to have some of that magic.

At 3 years old, I discovered fear and came face to face with it at the foot of my bed. I became like that cartoon character who would scream and run away from her monsters. Their shadows danced across my bedroom walls and sprang to life every night. My bedroom was no longer my fortress, and my monster wasn't imaginary. He became my reality. I was 17 years old when I finally broke free from a life of sexual abuse. I ran away from home for three days, the longest days of my life, hiding away from the world.

I found my voice and spoke my truth. I dug deep into the trenches of my heart and soul and dug up the courage to express what I had written in a letter to the person who had betrayed me, in a courtroom of familiar faces. With all the strength I could muster, I stood on the left side of the courtroom to advocate for myself. I transformed into a phoenix and rose out of my ashes. I left behind trails of hurt, shame, and guilt. I lifted my eyes and my arms towards the sky. As I rose, I saw a young child in the mirror, kneeling in front of the mirror. It was the little me! A child who may have had her innocence tainted, but nothing could steal the empathy, ability to love, or the forgiveness she held within her heart. That beautiful, little reflection of me smiled at the older, attractive version of me.

I saw hope flicker in the flames of her blue eyes and the determination as she stood tall. I had forgotten to extend my hand and remind her that after all she had been through, she was safe now. That child who grew into a beautiful, coura-geous woman was welcome because she would always be part of me. I took my power back and decided to use my story to empower others to grow into warriors, rather than settling to be just survivors. As I have gotten older, I have stopped searching for a bright light at the end of the tunnel. I realized that, all along, the light has been in every step I take. The light revealed itself as I walked through the layers that unraveled into my messy, vulnerable truths and the distorted lies were shed and left behind.

The many layers of my story have been woven together, connecting parts of me into a spiral of healing on this journey. Light has met each heart ache with a healing kiss. The broken pieces of my heart and open wounds in my soul have been sealed with love and grace. I have met parts of me with acceptance. Sitting posed humbly feeling unwrapped, exposed in my truths knowing these things were here to teach me. They were my gifts. I unraveled chains of shame from my ankles. The voices in my head took pleasure in seeing me crumble to the ground. I had to either feed my fears or feel them and walk on anyway.

Today, I stand here more than just a survivor. My story is a reminder of hope and a testimony of my resilience. It took me facing my fears and diving deep down into the abyss of my heart and soul to yank out the thorns and replace them with blossoms of victory. These chapters of my life are reminders of who I am. My story didn't settle in the ashes because I decided to rise. When I rise, I keep rising.

Some Days It's Hard To Open
By Kimber Bowers

A tear falls, expanding into a tiny imperfection on the crisp white sheet; just like all the perceived failures, the should haves, the could haves, of my miserably long young life spill out to taint the open canvas of this very moment. My mind weaves a million different worst-case scenarios. My body slumps under the weight of negative expectation and perceived loss. Pulling the covers over my head, I don't want to move. I want to stay snuggled in the security of soft, warm blankets and the safety of solitude. I am tired. I am tired from the heartache, tired from the struggling, tired from the unmet expectations, exhausted from all the running that doesn't seem to get me anywhere.

Have you been here? Have you felt this?

Unwilling to face another day, certain that I cannot take another moment, I burrow into the soft caress of my bed, refusing to open my eyes to the light – refusing to let in that light. I cannot bear another disappointment. I cannot risk another broken heart. There are jobs to do, demands to meet, and chores accruing that I don't have the energy to complete. There are illnesses to manage, expectations to fall short of, losses to bear, and bills to pay. There are disappointments to feel, pain to manage, and complaints to hear and I'm not sure I'm up for it. There are dishes to wash and people to take care of, and I'm not sure I know how. I don't feel like it, any of it.

"Wake up!" I hear my husband urge.

"I'm awake," I mutter as I pull the covers higher, waiting for him to go away, wanting it all to go away.

There are also people, he reminds me, whom I love, like a splinter of light in the darkness, that expands.

There are smiles to share, hands to hold, and hugs to embrace. There are pets to snuggle, growth to witness, flowers to smell, breezes to feel, seeds to plant, and adventures to take. There are games to play, music to hear, art to create, beauty to see, and touches to accept—touches that go so deep I cannot imagine never to have felt them. There are experiences for which I would not trade a single moment of my pain. There are connections for which I would live that pain a million times over in exchange. There are insights into grace and joy so rich that they are worth the risk, moments that might never have happened without surviving the breaks.

"You're not awake until your feet hit the floor," I hear my pappy direct from beyond the grave, and a sigh of deep knowing escapes my lips.

Light cannot get in until I open to it. All the stressors become doorways to a deeper experience. Every shadow becomes a window to light. Every loss becomes space for new gain. Every failure becomes a stepping stone to this very moment.

Every moment has the power to bring connection, wholeness, and growth (even the hard ones). Am I willing to step into this gift?

The covers come down—my weight shifts. Pushing to the bed's edge, I gingerly place my feet upon the floor. Focusing on this one moment and trusting in the growth that it contains, I open. I see the beauty of the highs and lows without needing to control it; this day will unfurl as divinely intended. Standing, I let light in, open to whatever blessing this moment brings; whatever form it is, I trust in it—open to receive.

Severed Parts
By Jeannie Church, MA

The first divorce recorded in the U.S. Colonies was that of Anne and Denis Clarke in 1643, in the Massachusetts Bay Colony. The first recorded in European history was the infamous divorce of Henry VIII and his marriage to Catherine of Aragon.

What caused the Clarke divorce was Denis abandoning Anne for another woman, with whom he also had children. Henry VIII's reason was that Catherine had not given him a male heir. Henry did not divorce his next wife, Anne Boleyn. He had her beheaded instead.

I want to be clear that I'm not a proponent of beheading as a form of divorce. However, the very word divorce means separation, severance, a breaking off. If you've ever experienced divorce or separation, you may have noticed that the act of severing an intimate relationship can feel sudden, like you are missing parts of yourself. Anne Boleyn lost her head.

My first two divorces consisted of me leaving them. This last one, my third marriage, my ex-husband broke it off from me. When he came to me in 2014 with the announcement he was attached to someone else, a total shock wave assaulted all my senses. Physically and metaphysically, it took all my effort to locate myself and my missing parts.

His timing could not have been worse. I was three months shy of completing my master's degree. The people in my life implored me to cross the finish line and complete my degree. I felt broken, but I did it.

I carved out time and containers for releasing hate, anger, fear, self-hatred, and deep sadness. Like so many others of divorce, I was faced with having to reinvent my whole self which in many ways was more challenging than the divorce.

Like the definition says, something had been severed, beheaded. Rather violent, I know. There were parts everywhere; body parts, heart parts, energetic parts, soul parts! Imagine them all in fragments desperately, slowly trying to find their way to wholeness again. The entire landscape of my life had changed suddenly as did the scene of my soul.

I began to realize the emotions, thoughts and all the fear releasing were not just for this man. It was so much more than only this lifetime. If I were looking in a rear view mirror, I would see I was given a strange, distorted, beautiful gift; I would have seen my karma racing towards me! I have come to know that the Universe had decided this was the way for me to make excruciating peace with my past. It was time to start reclaiming my severed Soul parts and divorce was the catalyst.

How did I ultimately overcome this deep-cutting separation? I followed the spark of my intuition and chose to remain in Colorado rather than return to California. I declared my time in Colorado as my healing journey with nature and time. I felt everything. I allowed myself to collapse and wail with grief—one ritual, one hike, one journal entry, one conversation, one therapy session, one breath and one day at a time.

As the veil lifted, I could no longer blame and hate my ex-husband. The focus had naturally moved from him to me and my betrayal of my Soul. It was a perfect storm for a wakeup call from Spirit, "Hello - Yes, this is Jeannie. Yes, I got your message, and I believe I'm now on track for full Soul recovery."

Life's Change's
By Tosha Fields

L ife changes for us in one way or another that can take us down a road of strength, passion, and ambition or a path of loneliness and despair. These changes can also bring us through any and all of the above and much more. For me, I have had many of those life-changing moments, but one of my most profound changes was the death of my mother and grandmother within a week of each other in the same year. There I was, a twenty-four-year-old woman with four siblings, ages ranging from eleven to sixteen. I had made a promise to my mother that if she passed away, I would take care of my siblings and that was a promise I intended to keep.

I knew nothing about being a parent, especially to four teenage children. My mother and grandmother died right before the holidays. Needless to say, Thanksgiving and Christmas were sad and challenging. We were still grieving in very different ways, but I didn't have time to fully grieve because I had to find us a place to live and figure out how life was going to continue without them. My mother's service and cremation were financially stressful as well. She did not have life insurance or money saved for me to make arrangements. It took everything I had to have her service and cremation performed. We didn't have family that we could rely on to help us. We were alone in this world. I knew

I had to do my best to make sure we stayed together. I went through the court and obtained legal guardianship to establish that we stayed a family. I reached out for help from everyone I knew and was turned down.

We were homeless for a while, then someone I knew was moving out of his studio and we moved in and continued to pay the rent. We tried to stay inconspicuous for as long as possible until I could find us a place of our own and a car. During this time, I thought that I had gotten in over my head. Mom had not been gone less than a minute and I couldn't even keep a roof over our heads. I felt that I had failed our mother, my siblings, and myself. I was determined to make up for my shortcomings.

I have Sickle Cell Anemia which is a genetic disease that causes the red blood cells to be sickle-shaped, and they are unable to carry oxygen. Because they can't carry oxygen throughout the body, it causes extreme pain and damage to any organ. I have no control over when a severe crisis will come or go. When they come on strong, I'm in the hospital, unable to work and be part of the continuous outside moving world and life. I didn't know how this would work when I'm unable to be completely present during those times. I could never fill my mother's shoes. All I could do was my best and hope that it would be enough.

I took things day by day, and I made mistakes, but I had to believe that my best would be good enough because I knew that not trying at all would be something I would regret. Embarking on this journey was something I did out of love and respect for myself, my family, and my mother.

The Land, The Sand, And The Labyrinth
By Linda Ingalls

In Sedona, I teach classes about energy. For one class, I use the Labyrinth at the wellness retreat center where I work. I loved the red dirt and rock that the Labyrinth was created from.

One day, the doctor asked if it was okay with me to put Sand in the Labyrinth so that people could walk barefoot. I thought, "It is not my Labyrinth, it doesn't matter what I think." When I eventually saw the white Sand, it felt odd. My eyes always noticed it when I passed by. I missed the red dirt.

Later, the doctor said one of the naturopaths had walked the Sand barefoot and felt it was toxic. He asked if I thought the Sand was toxic and if it should be tested. I was flabbergasted; how would I know?

Later, during my meditation, Spirit told me, "You need to perform a ceremony on the Labyrinth and bring the Sand into alignment with the Land."

"What the heck are you talking about? I wouldn't even know what to do!"

"Yes, you do."

"I do?"

I told the doctor, "Spirit told me I have to do a ceremony to bring the Sand into alignment with the Land."

He said, "Okay." I just love working with naturopaths!

I resisted. Then, one morning, I knew it was the day. Spirit told me to bring a baggie. I went to the Labyrinth but saw there was only chipped red rock around.

I said, "I don't know where any red dirt is." Suddenly, my feet turned, and I started walking. I felt disoriented, but I trusted and kept going. When my feet stopped, I looked down and there was a bunch of fine, powdery red dirt.

"Oh wow! Good job, Spirit!" I squatted, put some dirt into the baggie and stood up.

Spirit said, "Get some more." I did, then I walked back to the Labyrinth and stood just at the opening, holding the baggie.

I said, "Hi Sand, I need to do a ceremony and bring you into alignment with the Land."

A voice boomed out from the center, "Are you saying something is wrong with me?"

"Uh no, you're wonderful. I'm saying you are not in alignment with the Land."

"So, you think something is wrong with me!" It accused.

"Nope. Let me explain. The Land in Sedona emanates high energy vibrations that can uplift people's vibrations helping them to heal and come to a higher consciousness. And this is a Labyrinth whose purpose is to bring people's attention within themselves and help them to connect with their higher frequencies, and…"

"Ahhh, can I be a part of that? Can I do that too?" The voice now softly beseeched.

"Yes, you can! May I put a handful of you into this baggie with the dirt?"

"Yes." I put a handful on top of the dirt, letting them introduce themselves. Then, I mixed it all together.

"Now I am going to walk the Labyrinth and spread this mixture of you and the Land along the path."

While spreading the mix of Land and Sand, I talked constantly about the loving, high energy of Sedona and the power of the Labyrinth and how together they provided a powerful opportunity to uplift a person, resolve issues, increase consciousness, experience Love within, and connect to Love in everything. The words poured out of my mouth from a Source higher than me. I heard the Sand sighing; it felt overwhelmed by gratitude for this opportunity of synergy; to reframe and re-purpose itself.

Stepping into the center, I released the last handful of the mix. Suddenly, I saw the reddish, shimmering energy of the Land rise up through the Sand. I felt a soft caress and heard a sigh as they merged into one. Then a strong, powerful beam of light shot from the sky through me and into the ground. I closed my eyes and widened my stance to not fall. When I opened my eyes, I was facing the East, so I said hello to the East and allowed its energy to flow through me and down into the ground.

Spirit said, "Now turn to the South."

I protested, "Hey this isn't the medicine wheel."

"Just do it, Linda."

One by one, I looked to the six directions, allowing their energies to flow through me to the ground. From the sky, celestial and galactic beings sent their Love down. From the heart of the Earth and the nature spirits, Love was sent.

Spirit declared, "This is a Labyrinth in Sedona, where everyone is welcomed from all directions, from all beliefs, from all walks of life, knowing that *all paths are Love*."

I started crying, feeling the power in that declaration of intention and purpose.

I knew the ceremony was done. As I walked out, I asked, "Why me?"

"Because you heard, you listened, and you acted."

A week later, the doctor who'd said the Sand was toxic, re-walked the Labyrinth and had a wonderful experience.

Life Is Unfolding For Us And Not To Us
By Pedram Owtad

My heart was beating fast. I couldn't tell if it was excitement or anxiety. I heard my name and realized that it was time to step onto the stage to speak in front of 500 people, my very first public speaking engagement.

I stepped onto the stage, firm and strong, and while trying to see the audience through the bright lights blinding me, I found a moment of peace. I felt *all is well,* this is my message and it's my responsibility to deliver it.

Started my talk about my life and family story, but it was about one minute into my talk that I saw emblazoned in front of me on the teleprompter "…. (Pause)".

My mind ran wild. This is not the paragraph I have to talk about. Oh snap, where was I? Why does it say "pause"? That was supposed to be about two paragraphs later. Time passed. Okay, maybe the person who was supposed to change the slides missed it. Let's wait for a few seconds and she might realize and go back. Time crept by. No, apparently she's missed the whole slide. Okay, I'm fine. I have the whole talk memorized—where was I? Every second felt like hours.

I could almost hear the heartbeat of the audience, wondering, worried, questioning what's going on, or maybe they felt I got too emotional on this section of my talk.

I have to do something. I know this. I've practiced it dozens of times.

My mind went blank.

And suddenly, I heard one of the audience members scream: "We love you, Pedram!"

That woke me up. I thought to myself, "My notes—my notes." I turned around and as soon as saw my notes everything came back.

I continued my talk about circumstances in life that are constantly happening *for us* and not *to us,* and that we shouldn't get irritated, frustrated or agitated if things are not exactly as we want them to be, and once we find the miracles in everything around us, we are able to see life unfolding *for us.*

Backstage, after my talk, I was irritated, agitated and frustrated that everything didn't go as I wanted, and I was trying to find the cause and review what happened out there.

My younger brother, who was in line to speak a few speakers after me, reminded me that it was time to find the miracle in this difficult circumstance and "walk my talk." He also told me that the lady who was changing the slides backstage was very sad that this happened.

It made me wonder and realize—he was totally right! I must find what's in this seeming misfortune *for me.*

I reviewed the details. The big "…. (Pause)" on the screen in front of me hypnotized me. I remembered the lady who was changing our slides; a kind, nice lady with good vibes but seemed tired and heavy-hearted. Despite whatever might have contributed to her heaviness, she patiently changed all the speakers' slides for three hours.

All of a sudden, I remembered a nightmare that I had two weeks earlier where my PowerPoint was not matching with the coordinator's PowerPoint.

Wow! It was like the Twilight Zone.

So if I dreamed this event two weeks earlier, either:

I was stressed and I dreamed what I didn't want to happen, and as result, I thought about it and manifested it;

Or it was meant to happen and I was warned that I should be prepared for it;

Or it was meant to happen and I was informed that I can't do anything about it, so I would just go with it;

Or I experienced that dream to be triggered at the right time to let me know it was test-time. Could I really do what I'm preaching about?

That was the miracle that was happening *for* me.

In the end, backstage, I went to that lady. As soon as I saw her she started apologizing. I stopped her and hugged her. I told her about my nightmare two weeks earlier and that this was not her fault. It was beyond our understanding; either I manifested it or it was meant to happen exactly as it happened.

That hug and peace of mind were heavenly, and it was worth the whole past three months of training for this talk.

As my elder brother always says, real love is when we're giving it and we don't even know we're giving.

I'm grateful for every moment of my life, and I pray that we all become miracle-workers by finding gifts and miracles in everyone and everything that is happening *for us*.

A Deeper Call
By Rosemary Hurwitz

The professor who visited the Retreat Facilitator program on our last day surprised us!

He said, "After your two-year commitment to this program, you have received six credits towards a Master of Arts in Pastoral Studies at Loyola University." The coursework would combine Psychology and Spirituality; two subjects I loved.

As a busy forty-one-year-old mom and corporate recruiter, I thought, "I did this program for my volunteer work. I'm ready to deliver our fourth baby. It is a nice offer, but I'm probably never going to do that. As John Lennon said, 'Life is what happens when you are busy making other plans.'

Our beautiful daughter, Caitlin, arrived and was the complete addition to our family. I enjoyed her baby days and I continued to work, in part, from home. We had fun, and spent frequent Sunday visits at my aging parents' home an hour away.

When Caitlin turned two and a half, my mom passed away.

My sisters and our dad were at mom's bedside whispering our intimate final messages to her. My mom's passing was the only one I had ever witnessed and it was profound for me. I felt her spirit leaving her body.

I missed my mom, especially with a little one to enjoy together, but time heals the deep wounds of loss. I was getting our youngest ready for preschool when, suddenly, I had an urgent thought, "They gave us a five-year window for the Master's program. It's closing soon. I want to do this!"

My mom had been a strong spiritual influence for me. Having lost her mom when she was a child, she had developed a strong faith and passed it on to us kids. I have wonderful peaceful memories of lighting candles in week-day prayer at church with her. More importantly, my mom embodied her gentle calm ways outside of the church.

Knowing she was with me all the way, I was excited when the acceptance letter came for my Master's program. My husband and I were thrilled that I received scholarship money with four kids' colleges to save for; this felt like a sign.

I enjoyed each wonderful class: scripture, comparative religion, feminist theology and counseling. Now that I was enrolled in this program, what was to come from it? One windy day on campus, as I walked near Lake Michigan, I asked God, "How can I do this sacred work of spiritual direction with people when I am just 'damaged goods' like everyone else?" You see, I experienced acute clinical depression when I was in college and had carried the stigma of that diagnosis even though I became and stayed well.

I had grown so much from the experience and had much to offer others in their suffering. I was a wounded healer but way more healed than wounded. I heard deep within me an answer which still motivates me sixteen years later. It said, "I will put the words inside your mouth."

Loving my work in the holistic field, I've been published as a co-author in four inspirational books, and my first single author enneagram-themed book will be published soon. I thank the small soft voice within me, for its big guidance.

I am Enough, Right Where I am!
By Debra K. Rohrer

Weeks pass and the heaviness of the long day is here once again. The feeling of so much to do and not wanting to do anything moves its way through my entire being. Do I just go to bed or do I make some coffee and pound through the ridiculously long to-do list? The thoughts roam around my head as the night sky turns darker and darker.

The end of the day seems hard sometimes and my body feels heavy and my mind unwilling to be productive. Was my day wasted? Did I do enough for my job, my kids, others?

When do I take time for me? My heart needs something and I can't see clearly what it is. I'm frustrated and think about running from this overwhelming feeling. Is it loneliness that needs to be lessened? Is it that time marches on no matter what I do or don't do? Is it that the space between where I am and where I wish to be seems to be never-ending?

I choose to pause, breathe, let a few tears drop from my tired eyes. I venture deep into my soul to explore my humanness and the details of who I really am. I crack my home office window and let the cool night air rest gently on my face. Not so far in the distance, I hear the sound of an owl with its almost haunting call in the darkness.

I choose to accept all of me just as I am in that quiet or not so quiet moment of introspection. The vision I have of my journey is a beautiful thing resting gently in my mind. I see myself facing fear when it shows its ugly face, moving into the complete unknown when going back is unbearable, unconditionally loving my kids and dogs as they join me, trusting I can see the way to something better.

I make a decision to keep moving with an open heart and wide eyes. Always looking for the next right step,

the next positive thought,

the next place to give and

the next thing to be grateful for.

Each moment unfolds in its own special way. Tonight, I give in to the sleepiness and put something comfortable on. I find a warm spot to relax and feel confident with my choice. I tell myself, "I am enough, right where I am," and believe it!

Sensitive to a Technological World
By Lucy Sanford

It started with tingling, then numbness, high-pitched ringing in my ears and terrible insomnia. The tingling became a screaming-in-the-night pain, then electrical zapping in my head, like I was short-circuiting.

During the day, I could put my attention elsewhere, but at night, it kept me awake. I went to the emergency room a lot—CT scans, MRI's—but they could never find anything to which the neurological symptoms could be attributed.

Over the years, I became dizzy, nauseous and severely depressed. I developed chronic fatigue, Hashimoto's thyroiditis, sleep apnea, skin rashes, itching and burning. I couldn't remember things. My writing became dyslexic. I was extremely anxious and had bursts of anger for no reason. I was running on pure adrenaline and felt like an engine sputtering before it breaks down. I became suicidal. Two songs played relentlessly in my head: "Amazing Grace" and "In the Arms of the Angels." I was diagnosed with clinical depression and admitted to a psychiatric ward. I was given anti-depressants and anti-anxiety pills.

I was terrified.

It would take twenty years to discover I had a condition known as Electromagnetic Hypersensitivity. I had developed fifty-eight of the sixty-two associated symptoms and illnesses. I had become allergic to cell phones, WiFi, all wireless frequency radiation, electric and magnetic fields.

I packed my bags, dropped my career, sold my real estate business to my competition, moved to a small town where my mom lived, bought a house and gutted it for my condition. I felt okay when I stayed at my home. I couldn't go to restaurants, movies or public places. I'd dart quickly in and out of grocery stores. I spent a lot of time with my mom. We laughed a lot. I cried a lot. She'd take care of me when I would break down in fear for my future, which was often. She'd put my head on her shoulder and rub my back and tell me everything was going to be okay. Eight months later she was rushed to the emergency room. She died a few days later.

I spent another three years in isolation, exhausted from living in survival.

I discovered brain-rewiring and neuroscience. I'd visualize my new life and put myself right into that experience. I'd see, hear, taste, smell and feel it! It's our senses that tell the brain which chemicals to release; the ones to heal or the ones that keep us in survival.

I faced my fears. I traveled, took workshops and went back to school. I got certified as an Electromagnetic Radiation Specialist. I had just returned from my course in Santa Fe where I had trouble breathing. My teacher had said it was altitude sickness. My lungs were drained three times in ten days and I was diagnosed with Stage 4 Non-Hodgkin's Lymphoma. The biopsy showed that I had had Stage 1 and 2 for three to five years.

The Universe has its way of showing us the patterns and habits we need to change. I remember the "A-ha!" moment when I realized I had become addicted to being sick, to the stress chemicals the body produces when living in fear—it was when the oncologist told me if I didn't do chemotherapy, I'd die.

I felt pressured. I stopped listening to my heart. I questioned all the work I had done. I was angry and miserable. After two weeks of making myself feel sick, I had another "A-ha!" moment. "Oh my gosh! This cancer is a gift!"

And at that moment, I changed my perception and felt this massive dart of energy fly from my head into my heart. It was just after my first chemo treatment.

I went from Stage 4 to remission in just under three months. My oncologist was stunned, and my naturopath thought it was a miracle, but I now know that we are the miracle.

Acceptance
By Dana Lam

A recent sermon at my church was about the conflict we have with fighting for change or accepting what is. We are taught to fight for and work hard for the things we want in life. The opposite—accepting what is happening in our life—seems wimpy in comparison. If we accept what is, aren't we settling? Think about a time when you resisted something that was happening in your life. Did resisting make you happier? I'm quite sure that it made the situation even less tolerable.

I once knew a woman who was feeling stressed as a mother. As a divorced mom of two, she always seemed to feel conflicted. She loved her children very much and wanted to assist in shaping them into amazing human beings. She was nurturing and attentive to her children, but she was exhausted. The days her children would go to their dad's house, she had mixed emotions of relief and sadness. Welcoming the break, only to be responsible for herself, she felt an emptiness and longed for the two boys she loved so dearly. She was resisting being a mom. This resistance made her miserable. I'm sure it made her children miserable as well.

She was given a task to imagine her life without them. What would her life look like? What would she do? How would she live? After several days of visualizing this alternate life, she realized this was an impossible task. She couldn't imagine her life without her boys. It was in this moment of realization that she broke down into tears. It was in this moment she stopped resisting being a mother and moved into acceptance. In her acceptance of what was, she was able to find peace and happiness instantly. I know this to be true because this is my story.

Byron Katie, author of "Loving What Is," explains that it is not our experiences that make us unhappy but our thoughts about the experiences. The thoughts of wanting things to be different cause us distress. Is there something in your life that you have been resisting? When you accept things the way they are, you will be happier instantly. Let go of the resistance. Choose acceptance and bring on peace.

Every Precious Life Matters
By Vicki High

Who knew life would be such an incredible ride? I was born into an amazingly loving family. It was my "normal." Then life happened. People passed. Parents divorced. The lasting impact of change on my young life hurt deeply—I missed what I'd had. It seemed like I was absorbing the lesson to expect painful change.

Eventually, I married a man, a policeman who threatened and abused me. I couldn't call his coworkers for help. I could see my death reflected in his eyes and words. The pattern was there. I just failed to see how a "perfect future" faded to another "new normal."

Guess what? Somehow, miraculously, I lived. I thrived. PTSD kept me compartmentalized to survive, but I didn't realize it at first. Emotional connections equaled pain. Business success felt good. So, I focused on success and continued to be part of the walking wounded. I carried my burden silently. Decades later, I realized that I was so incredibly tired of carrying this burden, exhausted from trying to make sense of things entirely out of my control. I prayed and begged God to heal me from low self-esteem so that I could feel worthy.

As I approached 50, dragging the junk in my trunk, I know God blessed me and answered my prayer. In my heart, the Mini-Me and Draining Exercises were born. I sat in a swing along the banks of Lake Georgetown and did these exercises. When I rose out of that swing, I was a new person. These tools allowed me to excavate the truths I had that were buried beneath the avalanche of junk that wasn't even mine. I explored the unique creation I was born to be and loved her unconditionally. I dealt with the doubts and healed from the untruths. *I realized I was worthy simply because I was born.*

One of the greatest gifts from this experience led me to a bit of true wisdom for everyone. Each situation has both a burden and a blessing. When we are so fixated on dragging the burden, we can't see the blessing. The burden of domestic violence hid the reality that I was a survivor. I learned I could be fearless in the world because I'd already faced death and lived. When things seem really bad, I search for the blessing.

I was inspired to create programs that empower us to realize how we influence others. Each of us is a marvelously, beloved creation of God and unique in what we bring to the world. One message I received said it this way, "Before you were born, God kissed your eyes, kissed your lips, and anointed your soul." I believe this is part of each birthing process. I treasure the feeling I get that this happens for each of us.

Some people would think I am accomplished. I served as the mayor of my community and as a county leader. I appeared as a guest on the Oprah Winfrey Show. I had my picture taken with POTUS 43. The greatest creations come from being. As the founder of Heart 2 Heart Healing, I tap into miracles from the heart of God. With Empowered

Dreams, I help people live their dreams. With Kalming Kids, I teach and empower teachers to bring love into classrooms. I had to change my role as a "human doing" and remember I am here to be. I am a human being. I am here to live from the heart. I am a beloved child of God. I matter—everyone born and living on Planet Earth matters.

The Next Thing
By Barbara Womack

Once upon a time, a family decided to get back to basics, raise their kids on good food and somehow "serve the Lord." We were that family.

We were offered the opportunity of a lifetime, to live on a multi-generational farm. We had prayed and planned and then prayed a little more. It was so exciting to have this chance to raise our daughters in this type of environment. A lifetime of service, learning, and homegrown goodness seemed like a dream come true.

Until, that is, it all turned into a nightmare.

On a cold, gray February day, my husband and I faced down what I am pretty sure was the devil incarnate taking the form of my very own father. That wasn't part of the plan!

Everything changed at that moment when my father decided that he no longer wanted us on his farm or in his life. The hope, the dreams, the opportunities were all gone. There was no possibility of reconciliation when he made it clear he had no love in his heart for us at all. Maybe he had never loved me.

It was meant to be a leap of faith, not a plunge into a dark abyss. I thought we were changing zip codes, not everything about ourselves. It was the most frightening experience of my entire life. It seemed like the end of everything.

But, we had two small humans dependent upon us for everything. We couldn't curl up in a ball somewhere and quietly fade away. That was not an option. Our beautiful dream had come apart at the seams, and there was no way to repair it, to stitch it back together. We would have to find a new vision and figure out a way to implement it. We got up, faced the day, made a plan, and did the next thing.

I won't lie, it was hard. I cried and complained far more than I probably should have. My husband worked harder than he ever had. There were days when I honestly didn't think I had the strength to go on. To overcome any more disappointments, to put on a brave face, to somehow keep it all together and be a success.

There were so many things that needed our attention. Where to start? We start by just doing the next thing.

After a circuitous route, we found ourselves on a tiny piece of land in the middle of nowhere. We built a house, a barn, planted a garden. The to-do list was endless. So, do the next thing. Now, what about an income?

The fledgling "local food" movement was appealing. Small farms were purportedly better than big ones. And, we were undoubtedly small! Growing food was something that came naturally, and if we could provide for our family as well as help the world to eat better, so much the better.

Do the next thing.

We joined the farmers' market, a food growers' co-op, we put up food for winter. Our children were getting the education of a lifetime while we learned and grew together. Every day was full of new challenges and countless adventures.

From my vantage point of twenty-plus years later, I can look back and tell you that all the effort indeed paid off. Our daughters grew and flourished, and our business exceeded early expectations. We eat some of the most fantastic food ever (and so do our customers). The creative thinking required by all our problem-solving has kept our minds active and exposed us to new and exciting things. We were not defeated, we have indeed thrived.

Perhaps more pragmatic than inspirational, "doing the next thing" has served us well.

Weekends with Unicorn Driving School
By Michelle Forsyth

I've never been one to follow a traditional path. My non-traditional paths include an exciting (insert sarcastic tone here) time when I was 15 years old and became very ill with Chronic Fatigue Syndrome. I slept through the last half of my teenage years and even had to drop out of high school. But that's not what I'm writing about today.

Because of my prolonged illness as a teenager, I couldn't follow the traditional path that usually includes dating, learning to drive and activities associated with a North American teenage life.

When I was healthy enough to handle it, I wrote my General Equivalency Exam to get my high school diploma. I knew I would need that "graduation" date for going to college and getting a job later. I knew I'd get there; I didn't know when.

When I was 28 years old, my first serious relationship ended, and I had to start over. Not only was I recovering from a broken heart, but I also had to build my life from scratch. I had no money, no home, no job, no college degree, no driver's license, and of course, no vehicle.

I was able to move in with my dad and step-mother. They kindly gave me a place to stay and offered to support me for the unknown time while I got my life together.

At 28, I was starting where most 18–21-year-olds start. Most young adults have at least two years driving experience. I was more like a 16-year-old moving out on her own.

It was essential that I take driver training. We found Unicorn Driving School. Yep, that was what it was called. Luckily, this was an economical option and my dad willingly paid.

The instructor patiently understood my adult fears of driving. There is a serious advantage to learning to drive as a teenager when you think you're indestructible! Thanks to some family connections, I was able to land a job as an office manager for a construction company. Of course, falling into the non-traditional paths of my life, the job was not in the same city where I was living. It was one and a half hours away in a smaller town.

It was such a great opportunity, and I was extremely grateful for the chance to create a career. I took my driver's test. A few times. But no go. Literally. I passed the parallel parking portion on the first try (miracles do exist), but I was too nervous to pass the full test.

I worked and lived in my new town adapting to my job quickly and easily. Then, most weekends, I bussed back to the bigger city to work my way through 'Weekends with Unicorn Driving School.'

Finally, at Christmas, I passed the road test! For the first time in my life, at 28 years old, I had the tiny card that means everything. Freedom and independence were mine.

Dad gave me his old, but still decent, car. I now had income. A place to live, an excellent job, a driver's license, and a vehicle. Wow! In four months, I went from nothing to complete freedom. It was amazing!!

My dad asked me when I was coming to visit now that I had wheels. I was incredibly grateful for the help, but since no longer was I tied to 'Weekends with Unicorn Driving School,' I happily said, "See you in 6 months!"

Creating independence is possible.

Hope in Action
By Sophia Olivas

I cannot seem to recall a single day of my childhood that did not include father yelling at, name calling and demeaning my mother in front of my sibling and me. My first recollection of father was at the age of six months. I was lying in my bassinet when there was a commotion outside my room. I looked towards the source of the noise to see a male figure standing in my doorway, illuminated by the hallway light. The man, father, was yelling at my mother and man-handling her.

As the years continued, I learned to fear the rising sun. Every morning, father would come into the bedroom that my brother and I shared, and he would jostle us awake or yell at us. He always had something to say about what we did or didn't do the day before.

I had grown to fear father so much, that upon seeing dawn's first light and hearing father's heavy footsteps coming towards us, I would get so scared that I would pee in my bed. Upon seeing this, father would yank me out of bed and viciously whip me with a leather belt while shaming me. If I cried out from the whippings or made any attempt to protect myself, the more I was beaten. I was four years old.

At the age of eight, father was teaching my beautiful mother, who had a 6th-grade education, how to balance a checkbook at the kitchen table. My mother was not catching on quick enough for father, and I witnessed father smashing her face against the table while cussing her out and cursing himself for marrying a stupid woman when he could have married a hot redhead. I saw my mom's face, flattened from the impact and at that moment I decided that I would be happy. In spite of my childhood and all that had happened, I decided I would be happy, and loving, and I would thrive. I had hope for my future away from father.

In those tender years of my youth, I learned about the worthlessness of women, about what it means to be married, and to have made vows that included the words 'to obey.' I learned that love hurts, physically, mentally, sexually and emotionally.

At the age of 14, I found an opportunity when no one was watching, and I left home. For the next four years, until my 18th birthday, father would hunt me down.

Then I turned 18. Once I was legally free from father, I purchased my passport, grabbed a backpack and hit the airport. Since then, I have solo backpacked over 30 countries, generating friends all over the world. I have a treasure of precious moments spent being human and being happy. I run my own web development company, and I have spoken on large stages, discussing topics like how technology makes us more human and bouncing back from failure. I also speak in summits regarding violence. I have learned multiple languages, started a non-profit and I am writing a book about how Hope, combined with action and support, is the spark that evolves humanity and pushes us to greatness.

I believe in the importance of mental health. I am dedicated to continuous growth and development, including receiving constant assistance to deal with the fallout from the darkness of my childhood. I believe in love, and I believe in humanity. I trust life; I trust my path, and I trust the path of others. I recognize that being happy is a choice and I choose to be happy daily.

Coming Out Of The Closet
By Deedee Panesar

Yes, I have come out of the closet—the "Spiritual Closet." I am going to tell you the truth about my spiritual awakening, but first, you must know that I have been on the path for enlightenment since I was four years old. I knew then and had always known this was my path. But growing up in a Sikh background in a westernized Canadian culture all I wanted to do was to fit in society and be like everyone else.

For as long as I remember, I have had this inner knowing that I was here for a reason. In my early twenties, I had a calling, a purpose, but the whole thing stressed me out. It felt like I was walking around with this huge weight of responsibility on my shoulders. I turned to relationships, career, travel, food, drugs, alcohol and partying but none of them quite hit the spot. I tried traveling to the ends of the planet, in search for something that I could not find. I had spent the majority of my life looking outside myself for answers. Reaching for anything I could get my hands on, to soothe the subtle, aching, longing and deep calling within my soul which told me there was something I was missing, there was something more.

The harder I tried to hold it all together, the more I ignored the callings of my soul. The more I ignored the callings of my soul, the more out of flow with the Universe

I got. I was pushing, striving and controlling instead of listening, allowing and trusting. It took my whole life to come tumbling down for me to realize what I was searching for, was inside me all along.

Through my inner and outer crumbling, I have reconnected with the authentic light within. I am in the flow of the Universe. Mother Earth is calling forth a new awakening of consciousness for us to survive on this magnificent planet we call home.

We all start in spiritual kindergarten, and I am currently finishing spiritual high school, on my way to spiritual college. Before we can understand graduate school, one must understand the requirements of authentic, lasting spiritual and emotional transformation.

We each have a light within us waiting to guide us home. Our Soul Purpose is to shine this unique light in a way that only we can and in doing so, we spark something in another and inspire them to do the same.

My name is Deedee, and I am enough, just as I am, right at this moment.

Rising Again
By Rachel Gill

My heart aches

From every angle

I could keep turning it over and over

Those little cuts run so deep

Slices of light can be seen

Sometimes I wish there was an orajel just for the heart

A way to numb the pain

I kept searching

The tire gauge was in the corner

I wished for something to

Alleviate the pressure

It kept building up

I learned ignoring it only inflates it

Controlling it only binds me

It's an illusion

Thinking it's something I can contain

I found though when I let go

When I Rise, I Thrive

There was a relief

Surrendering was all I could do

A relief to be seen

Teardrops fell

Met the blue skies in my eyes

They began pouring

I realized that feeling the pain

Letting it be

Acknowledging it was everything

Numbness wore off

Though my heartfelt raw

Exposed

Vulnerable to the cold

It was no longer closed

Under an unnecessary pressure to be a certain way

I decided just to be

That's when my light began to strengthen

It's when I took that step back

Breathed again

Took my power back

It only mattered how I chose to react

That's when my world changed

When I Rise, I Thrive

Because I got up again

I rose again

The glasses I choose to wear

A choice to create

View the world

My story

Not as a victim

No woes

Just as a warrior fighting to create

The things that truly serve me

To live free from pain

No longer held captive

Just free to be and create as I learn

Each chapter

A choice to rise

Again and Again.

Saying Yes!
By Monica Brown

In 2014, I was a family-centered stay-at-home mom of three. One summer day, I left my children with their father and went to run errands alone. I had a cell phone, but I didn't use it. Anyone that knew me knew to call me at home. While out, I received a text from a local cafe owner, Cassie, whom I had briefly met in 2012. The text read, "Monica, I'm having an employee meeting. Would you come and guide us all in a short meditation?"

What?! I wasn't a meditation teacher. I had never led a meditation. I had only been meditating myself for two years, and she didn't know me well enough to know that! I was a trained Soul Coach and could do past life regressions and journeys. Maybe I could figure it out. I immediately said "Yes!" I thought that she meant that same day. She didn't. The employee meeting was the following month.

The next week I met with Cassie and Executive Chef Liz to get all of the details. They rarely had employee meetings. Cassie wanted to improve guests' experience and positively affect employees. She and Liz wanted the employees to understand how the energy they brought into the cafe affected everything for everyone inside the cafe and beyond. Cassie told me that I would open the meeting with a five minute meditation. She then left Liz and me to clarify the details. Liz wanted me to explain how the employees' actions affected guests, themselves and everyone, both on the floor and behind the scenes. I felt like I was getting mixed messages. Had I been asked to do a motivational speech or guide a short meditation? I reached out to Cassie. Her response was, "Whatever Liz says," and then she increased my time slot to 20 minutes. I spent several hours over the next couple of weeks fine-tuning complicated ideas and tools about life and energy into simple, easy to digest and use concepts and strategies to present at the meeting.

I wasn't a speaker. For years I had avoided being "seen." The day of the meeting was different. I was comfortable and confident. I watched the group as I conveyed my message. Weird, almost everyone in the audience was frozen and wide-eyed. Deer in headlights I thought! What had I done! I played it cool. I continued and closed with a five minute meditation. To my surprise, once finished I was surrounded by a handful of employees thanking and hugging me! I was confused. I left the meeting laughing not quite sure what had happened.

The next week, I was back at the cafe with Cassie and Liz. They were thrilled. The employees were excited about the information I had shared. They were trying out and loving the tools. I was relieved and glad that I had said "Yes!" Then Cassie said, "Wouldn't it be great if we had a weekly community meditation to raise the consciousness of the community?" I responded, "I would go!" Cassie replied, "Go? You are going to run it!" Within a couple of months, she handed me a key to her cafe. I led a weekly community meditation group accompanied by a mindfulness teaching for nearly the next two years.

In those two years, I learned so much! I naturally and unexpectedly stepped into my future profession as a presenter, motivational speaker, and coach. Saying "Yes" that day was a huge "Yes" to stepping outside my comfort zone and into opportunity, growth and more of my potential.

Shh...Listen to the Quiet Voice
By Monica Brown

I fought back tears as I sat across the table from my soon-to-be ex-husband. Our finances were too confusing for attorneys to deal with, so we had been advised to hire a financial adviser that specialized in divorce. The advisor we jointly hired as a neutral party was describing what she thought was the best agreement based on my husband's offer to me. There were a lot of details about the division of property and determining payment responsibilities.

I would be giving up most everything but receiving financial support. What I wanted was our family home. That was not an option. The house mortgage was almost equal to the support that I would receive, and the home was upside-down. He would keep the home, his business and most of our accrued possessions. I'd leave with my car, a wee bit of retirement and whatever support was decided in this room at this table.

I knew that I was fortunate. My situation was different from many others. I had created it that way. I would receive support; I was blessed. I was calm on the exterior but emotionally charged inside. I was a stay-at-home mom and leaving our family home felt like a violation. My very essence was in every nook and cranny of the property—my meditation area, micro-farm, and my love. Leaving was difficult to swallow, but a choice I made.

The advisor was laying out the length of support, taking into consideration tax consequences. He and I had already agreed on most items. She was recommending that spousal maintenance continue six months past our last child graduating from high school. Startled, my husband belted out "Why would I do that?!"

Until this meeting, I was confident in my future and my ability to create abundance on my own. But listening to the advisor lay out the details as she saw them was tough. Based on her projections, I wavered and fear crept in. I wanted to stand up for myself, say my piece. But there was a small voice in my head that said, "Breathe. Receive. Let him give this to you." I wanted to interject. She projected that his income with what we co-created would be vast by the time our children were out of school and mine would dwindle to zero. I knew that I had to reinvent myself and a new profession. I had been confident, but listening to her, I wavered.

He vehemently defended his position and encouraged me to disagree. I remained quiet, tears welling in my eyes. I was thinking, "How in the heck am I going to provide for myself and my children?" "Receive," I heard again. That was not something I was good at. I was learning as I moved through this divorce. I took a deep breath. Again, "Receive. Let him give to you. Receive." I relaxed my body, and I allowed breath to flow fully and deep. I relaxed my mind and stopped thoughts as they came in. "Receive."

Within a couple of minutes of me relaxing, opening and squelching the survivor part of me that wanted to self-protect, I was mostly calm. He was calming down too. The more quiet and relaxed I became, the lower his tone of voice became. His voice slowed until he agreed with the advisor. "Receive," I heard again. "Receive." As I relaxed, I smiled inside remembering that I had done this many times over the past couple of difficult years, and each time I listened there was grace.

Strangers In A Bar
By Kimber Bowers

It was another night in another bar, standing in the same restless spot that I had been in for what seemed like years. I could feel the destruction in my bones. I remembered how my deceased partner had thrown glass tables off the balcony in an attempt to break the monotony one night. He was looking for a "fix" in a sense to help him forget the ignorance he was living. And I understood how he felt.

Working long hours for little money to pay rent and doing anything I could to ignore the wasteful meaningless way I was spending my life in between. Somewhere I lost my passion. I forgot fury and excitement. And I was too tired from all the energy wasted on meaningless bullshit to see another way.

A man sat down beside me and asked why I was bothered. Another day had gone by, and I didn't even know what day it was, I explained. It was another day in a room without windows, without seeing a bird or sharing a laugh or taking a moment to lift up my arms to the sky and take in a deep breath and look at the clouds. Another day went by that I may have passed all these things and not had the time to see or experience them. Another day of rushing to make 600 pies to be thrown away, so wasteful, and I just wanted to do something *real*, something that was not against everything that is me.

"Don't make pies," this stranger advised me, "Whatever you do, just don't make pies." Don't make pies. It sounded so simple, but felt so complex. Baking was all I'd ever done. I was afraid that it was all I had to give.

"You are just factioned," the bartender said, and I don't think that's a word, but it fits. I was lost, misplaced, and presented with two choices: ignore my role, purpose, and path and be tortured by this ignorance falling deeper into self-destruction, or to place myself—pick myself up and go somewhere to be of love and service.

"Factioned," told me that the conflict was in me and that I was the one to fix it. I could not keep going and doing things because they were there for me to go and do. I now understood that life was meaningless because I was choosing to fill it with empty things; therefore, I was living and choosing recklessly to mask the hole in my life.

I left the pie man, my latest confidant, standing outside his door at the Quality Inn (strangely not irate that I had followed him to the door and then refused to go in). I also left my side view mirror dangling from a pole in a miscellaneous parking lot. I suddenly realized that if I sacrifice myself and my ideas of what is right and what my purpose is in this life, I might end up breaking more than a glass tabletop (drugs and alcohol taking their toll).

I left that bar, and I never went back. I chose to create meaning. I chose not to waste any more time or life or spirit. I chose to live not recklessly and blindly, but deliberately and meaningfully. I chose to see and accept the responsibility of knowing that there is goodness, truth, and beauty in the world. I would find my way to facilitate these things by stepping into my light.

I stood up and broke that monotony, without smashing anything, but a few lingering fears.

What's holding you back?

The Dance
By Andrea Sommer

y dad always says there are two things to be certain of in life. We die, and we pay taxes. You may laugh. But the truth is he's pretty much on the money with this idea.

We rarely think of our inevitable end, and it's pretty sad that we don't. For if we did, it would have quite a significant impact on how we live our day to day lives.

The truth is, I've been on this earth 47 years and have weathered many storms, but it hasn't been until recently that I've thought about what motivates me and what the hell my purpose is on earth?! The key lies in making ourselves the foremost priority.

"Let me fall if I must. The one I will become will catch me." —Baal Shem Tov

We must come from a place of love in complete adoration of ourselves in this crazy world, as energy is sensitive and cannot succeed in an acidic environment.

So one must push back and fall into solitude with one's self to find that passion. Stick with that passion, and not give a shit about what others think, as your life is *never* about them anyways.

How did I figure this out, you ask? Well, I have read my share of self-help books, went to therapy, gone to seminars, studied various healing modalities, observed those around me, and yet I was never finding myself fulfilled as this little voice kept nagging me. Listen to this little voice because, trust me, it only gets louder!

I have had many big falls in my life. The kind you'd think would have shaken me up enough to listen earlier. I had a cancer scare at 29. Left an abusive marriage at 37 with two children under 4, and one on the way. The following year, I lost two friends, one to cancer and one to suicide.

These are the experiences that rattle most people to the core and left me somewhat jaded, mostly due to frustration at not having pursued my own goals. The truth is at the very core of these lessons; I'd wished someone had given me the advice I'm giving you.

But in this world of niceties that exclaims, "Let's not hurt anyone's feelings, rainbows, unicorns, *love*—let's not push her off the cliff, what if she jumps?!" I never heard what I needed to. I had to learn it for myself.

We all have cultural and societal conditioning which says, "Be quiet, respectful, and responsible." Women and mothers are at the most risk of losing our identity. Don't misunderstand me; I'm not suggesting you hop on the next jet plane to help build a school in a far-off country and leave behind your responsibilities. However, I am saying it isn't necessary to give 100% to others in pursuit of what is deemed important in society.

So, here I am today, ten years later, in front of my computer typing this story to you. Still on my own, full-time with three beautiful girls, ages now 14, 12, and soon to be 10. I am beginning to be the mom and woman I've longed to become. I am someone who speaks from the heart, not concerned about the delivery, the expletives or taking time for myself to write. Many of us, as little girls, were brought up to believe we are complete when we finish a diploma-degree, get married, or have children. We think we are complete when we achieve that promotion or share our lives with a significant other. The life events we see in the movies are considered big things.

Sometimes the things that are necessary for our inner health are just small. It isn't about having a thousand followers on Facebook. It is this little burning flame inside you which is the most important. It is the flame that you will regret at your 95th birthday, or when you lay awake at night. We all came here to this earth for a purpose and, for the sake of our health, we need to listen to the yearning and take the necessary steps to see it to completion.

If we don't, it will manifest in illness and discontentment. Ancient cultures reference this energy that flows through us. Native American cultures name it Qi, and the Eastern cultures, Chi. When this life force becomes stagnated, it can produce illness and disease.

Spend time in nature to get in touch with your true self. Make a plan to achieve your personal goal. Your mind, body, soul, and your loved ones will thank you. For when you rise, we thrive as a collective!

Me, Myself and the Mirror
By Leanne Weasner

*"For all that I am, I owe to my
beautiful mother."*

As I walked into a small disarranged house, the smell of home cooked food and cigarette smoke always filled the air. Standing in the kitchen, tired and worn, was a woman of immense strength and grace. The woman was my mother, Brenda, my most significant role model.

Memories of my childhood echo through my mind, some I wish to remember, most I wish to forget. As a young child, I grew up watching the most beautiful soul live in sadness. Darkness had consumed her; self-love was not in her vocabulary; self-worth did not exist. She was love and kindness. She had no boundaries for all she knew was her golden heart and whom it beat for—Us. Always putting herself last, she slowly died piece by piece.

"One cannot foresee the love a mother possesses until she becomes the mirror."

As a young woman, I found myself looking in a mirror and saw my mother looking back at me. Tears ran down my cheeks. I saw sadness; darkness had consumed me, self-love was not in my vocabulary and self-worth did not exist. I knew I was comprised of love and kindness, but I had no boundaries. Always putting others first, I felt my soul dying piece by piece. A failed marriage and a young daughter to care for, I knew I had to break the cycle for I had little eyes watching me.

All Alone,

"Four walls and no windows my mother's thoughts had become mine."

I pushed through the pain from my past; black nights turned to dark days; my breakdown turned to breakthrough. With faith, hope and the Lord's light shining down on me; I slowly started to heal. Determined with a vision of my daughter's most significant role model in mind—Me. From broken to beautiful, my halo was placed on my true authentic self.

My Dearest Mother,

"God gave you wings to fly in heaven; you gave me wings to fly on earth."

As I looked in the mirror today as the woman God ordained me to be, I saw you looking back at me. I stood with immense strength and grace; I saw courage. I felt unconditional love for all and saw a beautiful soul full of kindness. I saw your sacrifices, but most of all, I saw the beauty you possessed. Out of the darkness, into the light; I thank you, my beautiful mother for teaching me the greatest lesson of all—to love me. I will shine in your honor and a piece of you I will leave, to all that cross my path—your golden heart.

To My Beautiful Daughter,

I see in you what I see in me. You're beautiful inside and out. You were blessed with many talents and gifts to share with the world. Your future is so bright like the stars in the night sky. You are comprised of love and kindness and possess a soul that shines. Always remember who you are and the beauty you possess. When the day comes, and you spread your wings and fly, always remember there is a piece of her in you that is in me—your golden heart.

"The key to your destiny lies within; the lock is in the mind. Courage is the gift that will unlock your greatest treasure, you."

As we journey through life, we hold on to so much emotion, mainly the pain. It is easy to forget the good times when the most damaging emotions claim our identities. I have learned that bad things happen to good people, it is a part of the journey. We can choose to live in pain, anger, and resentment or you can free your soul to accept, forgive, and choose love to be the greatest healer of all.

Loving yourself is the key that will set you free. I have learned that maybe this journey isn't about becoming who you want to be, perhaps it's about unbecoming who you have criticized yourself for believing you are. When you get knocked down by life, you must learn how to get back up and never allow life to knock you down again. Living through the pain and struggles I endured has made me who I am today. As the years pass, my beautiful mother becomes more of a memory, but one thing that will never leave me is her golden heart.

The Angel Coin
By Colleen Brown DVM

One late night in October, I had just returned home from a weekend trip to Sedona. Usually, I settle in from a trip before venturing back out. However, this night I felt a strong urge to go to the neighborhood grocery store. I was contracted to work at a local clinic the next morning and noticed I was out of milk. Since I needed milk for my morning coffee, I followed my intuition and caffeine addiction to the nearby shopping center.

The store was near empty with only one customer lane open. I got in line behind a gentleman already in the process of checking out. He was seated in an electric cart directly in front of me. Although I couldn't see much of his appearance from behind, other than his frame, there was something very familiar and comforting about him.

The man was having an ongoing conversation with the cashier about a coin. I couldn't hear the exact specifics, but it appeared he was trying to pay with a specific type of coin. All the while, the cashier seemed very perplexed. She repeatedly told the man that she wasn't sure if the coin held any monetary value and was therefore reluctant to take it.

I was intrigued, to say the least, and was concerned that the gentleman needed some extra change. I politely interrupted and offered to pay for his purchase. With the flick of his wrist, not only did he tell me "No" but he also nonverbally told me why I followed my intuition to go out at this unusual time on this night.

Santo Antonio Loparo was my grandfather who had passed away several years prior. He was a fascinating man with the best jokes and stories. There are many attributes I will never forget about him—one being his very distinctive hands. Whenever I think of his hands, I picture being a little girl in my mind's eye and watching him at his kitchen drawer fumbling with his wallet, in his basement workshop making beautiful stained-glass masterpieces or teaching me how to shoot pool like a pro. He had large masculine hands with thick fingers that always seemed to be curled precisely like the man in the grocery store. It was as if I was standing behind Papoo, as we use to call him.

Eventually, the kind cashier decided to take the coin as part of his payment and soon the gentleman disappeared into the night. As I approached the register, I asked her about the coin. She told me she wasn't sure what it was and left it at that. For a split second or two, I almost didn't follow my intuition and inquire any further, but I listened to the stirrings of my heart and asked her if I could see it. She pulled out of the register a beautiful shiny gold double-sided Angel coin!

Hebrews 13:2 reminds us to extend hospitality to strangers, for by so doing we may give hospitality to angels. There is not a doubt in my mind that the angel coin was meant for me. The cashier let me keep the coin, and it is one of my most prized possessions. To me, it represents a special message from my grandfather. The exact value of the angel blessing coins is debatable. For me, mine is a priceless reminder from my Papoo that I am loved, protected and will always live in abundance.

The Truth About Me
By Alicia Sweezer

The truth about me is that I'm different. I don't fit in the usual boxes, even though I spent a lifetime trying to stuff myself into them. I see, hear, feel, and know things that other people don't. This awareness doesn't make me better, just different and not 'normal.'

When I was little, I saw a movie, where a lady puts her hand on a young boy and heals his illness without telling him. I remember thinking to myself I would like to be able to do that for people. Little did I know that I was watching my future.

I've always known I came here to change the world, and I have carried that weight since I was very little. For many years, I turned off or at least turned down my gifts. When I did have an awareness of my gifts, I didn't know what to do with them. So many of my gifts are in tune with who I am and how I see the world, I am often unaware I am using them.

I always wanted to be a wildlife biologist. Animals and the earth are my 'thing.' Animals are just more comfortable to be around. They're quieter, calmer, and smarter than people. I was always 'good' with animals I just never realized that what I did with them was different than other people. Statements like, "My dog doesn't like anyone I can't believe he's asleep in your lap." Or experiences like having an elephant wrap her trunk around you while you both fall asleep in the back of the zoo truck became normal for me.

I had a successful career as a biologist, never really comprehending that I was using my gifts also. I thought everyone felt things the way I did; I thought that's how science felt. I am very logical, science-minded, and as it turns out, I'm very psychic too. I am a woman who has combined science and the mystical—who knew? Then, as a result of a series of injuries, my life took a significant turn and here I am today writing this story—something I would never have seen myself doing. I now stand before you as the being I came here to be. I live my life using my intuitive gifts to be in service and teach others (human and animal), and I change the world with every step I take.

Becoming who we are is not an easy path, it is the hardest path some of us will ever walk. And yet it is what we must do. Regardless of what others think, do, or say. Be the lighthouse you came here to be, stand firm and shine. I will not lie and tell you it is easy to be an Intuitive; it is not.

To know things about people that you might not have ever wanted to know and to feel the pains of the world is not always comfortable. To see the people close to you challenged and to understand why, and yet, not be able to help them, can be very painful and distressing at times. So, I wait with bated breath for them to choose a new way so I might be of help to them. For all the challenging times, there isn't anything I would trade for the times when I'm able to assist someone in healing and becoming happier. That is my purpose.

Now that you know the truth about me I invite you to speak the truth about you.

Getting Naked
By Tiffany Arenas

As I stood in the mirror naked, my thoughts began to get the better of me. "I'm tired. I don't want to do this right now. This isn't going to work." My husband asked me if I was ready, and with a nod, his hands began to caress my arms, my hands, my hips. He told me everything he loved about my body. I blushed and smiled. I felt connected and loved just the way I am.

As beautiful as this experience was, I want to love myself just the way I am. I am going to make different choices to get there. This is the year I am going to get naked—strip myself of labels, make different choices and take risks. I will be bold. I will be fearless. I will become me.

First, I chose not to be daddy's little girl. It was a Saturday night, and I answered his phone call despite something telling me no. "I want to talk about our relationship," he said. I felt my stomach churn. The conversation played out as it had many times before over the last four years. First, he played the victim. Then, he attacked. Then, he played the victim again. What was different about this conversation was that I listened to my feelings and made a different choice. I never wanted to feel this way again. I told him I was hanging up and clicked off of the phone while he was mid-sentence.

I immediately felt relieved. I was proud of my decision for a few days until an e-mail appeared in my inbox. The title said it all: "Your actions have broken my heart." My dad is not able to love me for who I am, and that is okay. I chose to surround myself with those who do love me for me, and that does not include him. One day I will be completely confident about this decision. Until then, I choose to heal without him in my life.

Second, I will no longer be a manager or a leader. One day, I received a call from my supervisor saying that the assistant director was in a new role effective immediately. I felt anger. I just figured out how to accept her approach and not take her actions personally.

For months, my staff and I were in the hot seat. Anytime a parent or community partner complained, we were not given the benefit of the doubt. She did not care that the process was broken and the resources we requested for years were not provided. Harsh emails and conversations led to tears and sleepless nights. "She's been this way for years," a colleague said. "She does this to everyone," another one said. Why is this okay? Why would my organization allow people to treat one another this way? We help the most vulnerable people in the state yet we cannot provide a loving and supportive environment for staff. I choose not to be in such an environment and not be in a high-pressure position. I choose to take a risk—quit my job—and find a position that brings me energy, where I am in a supportive environment.

Getting naked will require that I take risks and make different choices. I don't know what the future will be like, but I know that a shift has happened for me and I am ready. This is the year I get naked, and I become me.

No Longer Bound
By Rachel Gill

I woke up this morning

Shivering as my icy truths were

Numbing the deeper parts of my soul

I felt like a prisoner to so many lies

I slowly begged my body

My fingers to crawl

To reach out and peel back a single

Layer at a time

I'm frozen in time

Paralyzed by my fears

I can't feel my feet when they finally meet the floor

So numb

Almost feels like I'm walking on air

I reach the mirror

Sink down on my knees

The cold invading me

I begin to weep

When I Rise, I Thrive

I have to look up

Oh that face in the mirror

So beautiful

Such fierce blue eyes

Tears spilling

Little oceans of determination

I can't bear to take my eyes off her

For fear of losing her

That girl in the mirror is still a part of me

Before the wounds began to soak her heart

Before she grew to know despair

Endless nights wrapped in someone else's presence

Tainting her innocence

She becomes just a memory in the mirror

Who she once was is no more

Oh I never wanted to leave

I couldn't stay

My hands bound in pain

It left me scared to fight

As I begin to drift away

I search for comfort in my mind

Metal stings my wrists

When I Rise, I Thrive

My ankles

Something sharp grazes my skin

Enough pain to pierce my heart

I want to break free from these chains

Salty tears infused with dirt

Memories holding me captive

My search for freedom

Quest for worth

Can I ever be free?

That face in the mirror had once held hope

Before my world was smothered in darkness

Tainted

Feeling my worth slip away

I had felt so deserving of a beautiful life

At that moment, I saw in my mind

What it felt like to not be shackled by my doubt

Held down by another man

Pinned in a corner

No way to flee

The shame I felt that night

A secret basement of lies

I stumbled down the stairs

My feet bare

Not stopping

Glass crunching beneath my toes

Metal begins to snap

Oh, I will break free!

Light dances across the darkness

Something shiny reflects an image

I run free

The mirror holding my younger reflection

I hold her gaze

Knowing connects us in our souls

I have become free like her

Free like before when my world was more

Than just a dream.

Free

No longer bound to the chains of my past

Whole Again
By Rachel Gill

I ignored her phone call today

I couldn't bring myself to answer

My tone would tell it all

So I stared at the phone

I couldn't find the strength to face the pain at that moment

The grief was so thick

Stuffed down so deeply

I was afraid it would bleed

As I began to pull it up

It fractured into thousands of pieces

Slivers of light shining through my chest

Aching cuts against my soul

For so long

I've let the voice of someone else

Quarrel with my heart

Like a virus spreading across my mind

So reluctant to assert my voice

If only I had awakened from my faintheartedness

When I Rise, I Thrive

Sooner

I grasp for the only thing I can

My form on the floor

My soul is so wearied

I've given my all

I can't take the noise

I've poured all the light

The love for someone who will never understand

They chose to ignore my voice

That's okay

I can barely utter a sound

Dark clouds are hovering over me

Ready to unleash its furious army

It's just me and my shadow

I rise

As I walk the line in the sky

My soul begins to breathe again

I haven't failed

Every lesson has informed me

Inspired me to see my greater purpose

Such luminous light

Suppressed for so long

Brilliance from my soul as it meets the sky

When I Rise, I Thrive

Igniting it on fire
Strength searing through me
As I ascend higher
Until my heart begins to heal
Making me whole again.

Heart Song
By Rachel Gill

Like Oxygen to my soul

I dance across the sand

Effortlessly in the wind

Soaring through the air

My heart is free

No chains on me

As I dance, I feel the song

Deep within me

Ever so gently

It begins with a whisper

Only I can hear

As I fly, I cannot hide

Continuing to soar

My heart calls out

Ocean waves become my song

A song I must embrace

I will not stop dancing

Though the waves are high

I'll begin with my dance

Along the sand

Let my dance carry me like love over the waves

Let the love consume my soul

The dance, the power to take me higher

Take back what is mine

Waves crashing through my path

Will not knock me down for long

I choose to dance

I choose to soar

I will not be reduced to a lull

I will listen to my heart song

Let it call my name

Keep dancing

Only my dance is in my power to control

I will leave the shallow place

Let myself brave the deep

Keep dancing

I will not become just a glow beneath the sea

I will be a dancing flame

Roaring strength

Not giving it the power to pull me under

I will be strong

I will not let someone else's song become the only music

The only voice in my mind

My song will spread like fire across the sea

My dance

My heart song will keep me free

Phoenix Defying
By Karista Rose

The mythological phoenix bird has a story with many different versions across cultures around the world. The one consistency is that the phoenix, defying the odds, always rises from the ashes with a new life. My life experiences have caused me to identify with the story of the phoenix.

I first became a "phoenix defying" at age 12. I survived 12 years of daily physical abuse by my mother. Child Protective Services gave me a new life, and I thrived. Several major experiences have occurred over the years, connecting me to the story of the phoenix, defying the odds, and thriving each time. In fact, "Defying the Odds" is my mission statement.

In the fall of 2017, I rose from the ashes again.

I have migraines, hypothyroidism and adrenal insufficiency—a rare, daily life-threatening condition. I once went to the hospital, thinking I had a migraine. After being given the usual treatments, I was still extremely sick. Unable to keep medications down, including my daily life-saving adrenal insufficiency medications, I was told I would be admitted. That was the last thing I remember.

Next, I awoke in a brightly lit room with hospital staff rushing around me. I tried to move my hands towards my mouth. They were held down. I was told I had a tube helping me breathe and was in the Intensive Care Unit. Later, I learned I had had a code blue called. I had slipped into adrenal crisis and the very rare myxedema coma (no thyroid hormone in the blood). These combined issues are usually fatal. It was a miracle I had survived. I almost died that night. My son would have been without a mom; my husband would have lost his wife.

After everything happened, I had to work physically and mentally to cope with the trauma—the shock that it happened and that I was still alive. I had nightmares for months, and I was frightened to close my eyes for fear I would never open them again. I could have chosen to continue to live in fear. At any moment, it could happen to me again, since my adrenal insufficiency and hypothyroidism are permanent conditions.

During the week I coded, I was supposed to be in a beauty pageant competition. After surviving my code blue, instead of forgetting about the competition altogether, I chose to continue chasing my dream in 2018. I grasped and cherished every opportunity that came my way, both for the competition, and to be an example to other future phoenixes.

During the competition weekend, I knew I shouldn't have attended. I cherished every moment, regardless of whether it was good, bad, frustrating, silly or sweet. Every moment meant I was alive and breathing. There were the usual awards and crowns (who doesn't love and want those), but this phoenix had already received her award by rising from the ashes.

I earned most of the awards I had worked towards, as well as a couple of surprise awards. I didn't win the division I had entered, but I completed my goal of competing. But it didn't end there.

There was more than the one competition that was being judged. It was considered the hardest to achieve due to the requirements that had needed to be met throughout the year. You were competing against all the other contestants as well. I was unaware of this and cherished the honor and moment of being crowned. "Defying the Odds" I truly felt I was thriving like the Phoenix.

Who's Going to Love Me?
By Shamegan Smith

I've always been different and never fit into society's standards. I believed I was doomed from birth. With a physical ailment, the inability to walk and a bad stutter, I was unable to speak. What did I do to deserve what happened to me? I grew up to be more than everyone expected me to be, but it still wasn't good enough for me. Due to the countless times I was teased and taunted, it left me wondering, "How could anyone ever love me?"

I could now walk without braces and talk without stuttering, but I wasn't good enough. If I could only be normal, people would accept and love me. I grew up to be an adult not loving myself, so I began to buy love because it did not come freely. I realized my family, associates, and men I would meet treated me a certain way when I paid for their time and love. I made myself into this successful person who appeared to love herself and have confidence so that I could buy love.

Inside, I was this broken little girl that was handicapped. As time went on, I became even more broken because the love I was receiving was not authentic and I didn't love myself. I set myself and others up for failure with false expectations. I would get angry when they didn't show me the love I wanted because I am paying for it, by sacrificing. I'd give to people, even when I didn't have it. I wanted love, and I would get mistreated when they were done using me. I realized I don't love myself, never loved myself, I had no clue of who I was, and didn't know how to get the love I needed.

I began to break down bit by bit, and put the mask on around mixed company. I didn't realize I had become a stranger to myself. I would get upset at others because they couldn't love me as I needed them to.

Throughout this time, I remained a stranger and continued to buy love. I was robbed of two children by miscarriages and countless years of heartache and failed relationships. I ran every time things got hard, and I was hurt. I moved four times to three different states to escape the hurt that I caused myself with false expectations. I felt damaged beyond repair. I couldn't understand why I was in bondage. I believed in God, why was I still suffering?

The key was I didn't trust Him and allow Him to heal me and show me how to love myself. I began to go through the process of becoming consecrated in Him. Through becoming consecrated and centered in Him, I began to learn how to love myself. I started creating boundaries and stopped enabling people. I didn't feel guilty anymore about putting myself first. I stopped buying people's love and let go of the sense of needing to feel wanted by others. I was such a good person, but the method of purchasing love was a way to manipulate others to get what I needed and still didn't get what I truly desired.

It took me so long to open my eyes and realize the part I played in my story and not becoming whole. In my self-discovery, I learned how to love myself and others unconditionally. I know the true meaning of unconditional love. I use that knowledge to continue to help myself to inspire and encourage others so they might become advocates for themselves working toward becoming whole.

Moving Past Limitations
By Nell Jean-Mitchell

In my heart, I feel I am the smart, sassy, outgoing, young, southern girl of my youth. But my outside mirror shows quite a different picture. There, in the reflection is an older, aging woman with a bent frame from scoliosis, little rolls here and little rolls there, a face of smile and worry wrinkles, blind in one eye from early glaucoma, a severely scarred leg from skin cancer, fingers bent and deformed from arthritis, and graying hair every 30 days until I get my 'touch up.'

This area of body image and aging may be shallow even to be considered worthwhile thinking or writing about. But as I reflect on my life, I feel I have always been a successful woman who thrived on first being a loving, and caring mother providing a home full of laughter and unconditional love, as well as balancing family as a successful educator. I have overcome many obstacles and tragedies. I could stroll in any place head held high and in a short time, meet new people, lead an educational workshop, contribute my knowledge to the occasion and feel I had made a difference. Now, wherever I go my height is reduced, I walk much slower with a slight limp and concentrate on seeing where I am. I fight the panic attacks I feel rising when I bump into things in a crowd or can't find where I parked my car.

How do I feel good about myself and thrive with joy? By being a positive role model of aging for my family. I have dug deep in my heart and reflected on life's beauty, and joy. I am determined to love every minute I have left. I thrive on birthdays to come and celebrations to be enjoyed! I fight any depression that comes my way. And I refuse to be or play the victim over physical limitations!

I love birthdays and holidays as much as my mother did. She used to say in her sweet southern voice with a little giggle, "It's always better to have a birthday and holiday than none at all, because you would be dead!" I choose the alive path to make days special. I surround myself with positive, loving family and friends. I seek classes that uplift me. On extremely physically painful days, I stand in a hot shower and repeat mantras on what a great day it is. When I look in the mirror and dab makeup over my wrinkles, I'm thankful there's a lot of happiness and laughter going on there!

I appreciate and love myself for who I am and continue to strive daily to be a loving, happy person. I am thankful I wake up each morning and enjoy the day. I can still laugh and play with my two-year-old grandson and experience the joy of his daily learning. The days my bent fingers can't play the piano, I can love his attempts of trying to learn or dance to music on the radio. If I can't see well, I look for a marker to guide me. I stay ahead of my limitations by planning and making arrangements so that I can be independent. And I am ever so thankful for two children and a grandchild who loves me unconditionally and a supportive, positive husband who loves me just the way I am and still calls me his "curvy cutie" even though the curves are bent. By loving myself inside and out, I am embracing the aging process with sheer determination, strength, and dignity.

Surround Yourself With Good People
By Giuliana Melo

"It's our job to teach people
how to love us." —Sunny
Dawn Johnston

It is said you become like the five people you spend the most time with. To thrive, I had to decide who were my people? What goals, dreams, and desires did I have? How was I going to get there? What did I have to heal to become more? See more? Be more?

After a walk through cancer, I knew that I had to do something. I had to take a good long look at where I was focusing my energy. I had to find teachers that resonated with me, and I had to find friends that supported my growth.

One day I saw a post on social media that said: "Surround yourself with people who will lift you higher!" Wow, that resonated with me. I knew that meant that I had to discern what kind of events was I going to and what types of classes was I attending.

I began to follow my intuition. Intuition is that little voice from within that guides you in the right direction. I let go of people, places and things that hurt me or that were drama-ridden and instead surrounded myself with the doers, the motivators and those who inspired me to become better. The energetic vibration of competition doesn't feel right to me, so I found a teacher who taught me how to heal, learn, grow, and expand my life. I learned that I am so much more than what others thought of me and that I had the power to change and manifest dreams.

Some of the things I did to heal my life were:

• Left a 32-year career to pursue my love of all things Divine.

• Learned to heal with the angels.

• Studied mind, body and spirit principles.

• Learned about the power of the mind and how positive thoughts change your life.

• Learned about grounding and protecting my energy.

• Learned to meditate.

• Prayed regularly.

• Started a gentle yoga practice.

• I wrote about my experiences.

• I found my voice and began to speak at events.

• I added creativity and beauty to my life.

• Pursued Goddess healing studies to ignite the Goddess power within me.

• Empowerment coaching and learning my archetypes so that I could heal them and become more woman energy.

It takes a village to heal, and I knew that I thrived with a community. I learned community builds immunity and I immersed myself in my mentor's communities. I now fill myself up daily. I heal continuously, and I ask angels for help with everything.

God has been my anchor. Faith is my lifeline. Angels are the support I needed and wanted. I learned that because of Divine free will I had to ask for help. That meant I had to become a better receiver, as I was a great giver. I had to ask my family, friends, teachers, angels, and God for help. I ask for Divine help as a daily practice.

To get out of the victim mentality to rise and thrive, one must dig deep and make choices they never had before. You must be committed and consistent in your healing. You can do it! Set an intention and decide you are worth it. You only get this one journey we call life. At any time, you can make a choice. What do you choose? Do you see life as the beautiful opportunity it is? Do you believe life happens for us and not to us? I had to shift my perspective. I can see the magic in life, and now I expect it.

When I Rise, I Serve
By Kim Clayton

I always wanted a life of service. I started that service by running nursing homes right out of college. I proceeded to do crisis management of the most troubled homes for many years. I worked seven days a week and often 16 hours a day. I didn't care for my body, just the mission of serving others. I maintained an incredible pace and stamina for so many years and was a young rising star. Then, I was thrown off the gerbil wheel at full speed when I acquired a chronic illness so severe that I could no longer work. I suddenly lost my identity and purpose which was rooted in my work. I am still learning that these years of illness have been a silver lining or blessing as I would never have stopped to connect more fully to my purpose and destiny. Trials are intended to help us walk through difficult lessons and bring us closer to God's alignment with him.

Though challenging, the choice is always: I can give up, or I can get up. As much as I hate to admit it, daily tasks once so easy are sometimes a battle, but I have realized that even in the valley of pain, service is a reason to live. Through deep, unspeakable despair and pain, I found that connecting with those in need, helping fill a need in any capacity sustains me if only breath to breath. Service fulfills my deep human need in a way few other forms of action can, regardless of how large or small the mission. I am still learning to accept that the mission may not be massive, but every act of kindness, every interaction with living beings creates an opportunity to serve. I am able to express love and compassion, which gives me joy.

I see now how service is love in action. While I always was a giver, I never considered any of my small acts of goodness any more than that—small. I longed for, and still do, great missions where I can help many. It was never unusual for me to feel bad seeing a homeless person with no coat visually distraught and braving the elements. It was not hard to give that person change, or an old coat I never wear. The same applies to animals. To me they are equal. A new cat showed up on my deck, abandoned by someone. He was crying, and I could see his ribs. I gave him food, water and created a little cat shelter for him where he sleeps. In the hospital, on a gurney, I was in pain, but it came in waves. Another man was parked across the hall from me, in acute pain. He was crying, scared, and alone. I got off my gurney and went to him. I placed my hand on his shoulder and taught him how to breathe to bring in a feeling of calmness and helped him to not feel alone for the time we were together.

I still struggle to believe these little missions are enough and I crave a great one. It does not always seem to be enough, but to the hungry, thirsty, scared souls it was everything they needed at that time, and who would have done it if not for me? For now, these are the missions, in composite, which will amount to a great one. Sometimes the trial we so loathe is the very mission we must accept and embrace before we can be given an even greater mission.

How I Got Through
Something Really Scary
By Isaac Bowers

My mom can get knocked out sometimes, so I have to take care of my sister, Ciara. When I get scared, Ciara flips out; and when Ciara flips out, I start to flip out, so it gets kind of hard to take care of my mom.

One evening, I was on my computer when my sister Ciara came and said, "Mommy is laying on the couch. She won't wake up!" I could see she was scared and knew this was serious.

When I got downstairs, mom was laying on the couch making grunting noises. I tried to wake mom up by talking to her and shaking her, but nothing worked! My heart felt heavy, and I started to freak out. What would I do without my mom? If something happened to mom, dad would have to work, and no one would be here to take care of me. Mom's the one who feeds me, helps me fall asleep, settles arguments with my sister, calms me down, cares for me when I'm sick, and makes me feel good inside. Nobody does these things quite like mom.

I was scared, but I knew it was probably her blood sugar, so I thought of what to do next and called Dad on the Echo. When Dad didn't answer, my heart dropped to my feet. I was breathing hard, unable to get enough air, unsure what would happen and afraid of what could go wrong. The more I got scared, the more my sister got frightened, so I tried to stay calm. I saw my mom's phone on the table and called my Grammy.

Grammy told me to give Mom juice, but Mom kept spitting it out. She wasn't waking up, so I told Grammy I would call 911. After explaining to the dispatcher what was happening, I gave them our address and waited for them to come.

My sister, who is only five, was yelling and crying because she was afraid and I realized that with my mom passed out, I would need to be the one to take care of her. I started thinking about what makes her happy. I know that she likes snake videos, so once the paramedics arrived and I knew Mom would be okay, I took her upstairs and put on some snake videos to take her mind off it and keep her calm.

I kept going downstairs to check on Mom and was very relieved to see her wake up. I love my mom enough to fill an infinite void, and I was so happy to know that she would be okay. Having Mom in my life makes me feel like my world is secure.

From this experience, I learned that even when we're scared, we can still be brave by calming ourselves down and focusing on just one step. Even though I was frightened, I took the steps needed to help my sister and my mom. I am now very proud to have a certificate of bravery and Medal of Honor awarded by the county for remaining calm enough to give them important information in a scary situation. I am also very thankful to have my mom and will let her know that every chance I get.

Next time I am scared about someone's safety, I will remember to stay calm and focused in order to get help. Next time I want to tell someone I love them, I will tell them right away.

What I Learned
By Rosalie Weatherhead

My story isn't fascinating. I want to say thank you to all of the people who were great teachers. I know many people have encountered terrible trauma and horrible experiences and my heart cries for them. If I can help them, God knows I will. I do know this much is true: I don't help everyone anymore. I understand that everyone is on their journey and sometimes pain makes us change. My life has not been horrible, but it's not been roses. I married a man I didn't love because my parents told me I had to be out of the house by age 18 and he wanted to marry me. I didn't know he had a mental health problem, well, problems actually. It took a while to leave.

I walked down a mosquito-ridden dirt road with an 8-year-old girl on the one hand and a 9-year-old on the other hand and I realized that there was nothing behind in the house worth ever going back. That baggage went with me to my second marriage. But he didn't respond to my flailing and wailing and craziness that was spewing from the victim in me. He loved me. I had so much to learn. He has been patient and accepting through my journey.

This article is to thank some people for the lessons they taught me. First, I want to thank my mother. I no longer am angry at the things that I experienced. I am grateful because I am an excellent mother because of her. She taught me how not to behave, how not to treat others and how horrible it is for those who endure it.

I am thankful for my first husband. He taught me how to be more organized, how to recognize when someone is acting out in an undesirable way that it is "not my monkey, not my circus." I learned I didn't have to own another person's bad behavior and love someone who wasn't capable of giving or receiving that love. I am grateful for the two beautiful girls he gave me, whom sadly he knows very little about.

I am also grateful for the boy who got me pregnant at 17, who decided not to marry me because he was not mature enough for a relationship or a family and neither was I. Thank you for teaching me you can love someone who doesn't love you back and that's okay.

I'm grateful for my father who loved me deeply and completely but who had some bad moments. He taught me that he could be a good father but not such a good husband, and being a good father was all that mattered to me.

Unconditional love is accepting our family and those we take as our family. Even our psychotic sister, who had violent tendencies and who is 71 years old now, her journey has thankfully brought her to find love and peace.

I want to thank all of those who spontaneously scream at me about something that could be said much more easily, much quieter. They taught me to stand still and let them fizzle out to the point where they can become aware of their actions, and I never have to say a word.

When I rise, I thrive because I take a little gold nugget from every experience. Lord knows, I don't want to have to go through it again. Sometimes that brick wall I keep smacking against while I'm learning becomes too familiar! I am a person more whole and complete because of the things I endured and because God is molding me, making me into something better with every experience!

Empty Spaces
By Kimber Bowers

Somehow I always get back to a place where I forget that empty space ever wasn't terrifying. A blank canvas or a page like this one, an unfilled day, a new experience, an open future—they are all the same.

When I was younger, I flew right into them without even thinking. Present and ready for adventure—open arms, open heart, open mind. There came a time when I began to pause, to question, to look for evidence, to not trust what I found—to doubt. Disappointment and hurt are hard teachers. These things happen, but better things can happen, too.

As an adult, I sometimes forget the value of any experience. I wanted to sit down here and write something inspiring; but the blank screen before me was daunting, and I was not sure where to start. "What if I have nothing to say?" "What if no one learns anything?" "What if it's not good enough?" "What if I'm not good enough?" It's the same old story.

It's my fear; my mental composition of all the 'shoulds' and the doubt that I'm enough to meet them, that holds me back. There are times when I look out over the vast horizon and see endless possibility. Then I look out and see a vast expanse of nothingness that seems to stretch into eternity waiting for me to fill it. I don't know where to begin. I expect to mess up, so I don't. I forget to be open to the experience now.

Fear is the thing that keeps me playing small and whispering. Fear is the heap of unpublished manuscripts buried in my closet. Fear is the memory of an experience that prevents me from being open to a different possibility. Fear is a lack of trust in the unknown. Fear is the discomfort of growth. Fear is the self-locked shackle that keeps me from being all that I am. Fear is natural and ebbing, like all other emotions, a wave that rolls out just as quickly as it came in and I can learn to surf it.

I realize that no matter how many times I feel like I'm shattering through my fear, there still will be another layer. Fear always pops back in. I've been looking at my life and what I am creating and insisting to myself that the fears have been released and that nothing is holding me back, but I'm still not getting where I want to be. Yes, I have worked through a lot; and yes, there's even more growing to do. Growth is an ongoing process. And fear is a natural part of the cycle. It doesn't make me any less to recognize a few more fears.

Maybe it's not about shattering fear. Perhaps it's more about accepting the fear and integrating what we can learn from it.

Sometimes old fears resurface; sometimes new fears spring up. Being apprehensive is okay. Being afraid is okay. Being a little resistant is okay. Allowing the experience is okay. Life is a process of balancing it out as we recognize the fear and embrace the excitement gathering the strength to keep moving through it, gaining the trust and finding the freedom we crave. We cannot find that freedom, without first acknowledging the fear for what it is. Acknowledge fear and choose to do it anyway, open to the lessons. The more I integrate this, the more my life changes, all in good ways. But I'm not done yet.

Does anyone know a publisher???

An Act of Self-Love
By Dana Parker

I used to think that if I worked hard and did my best, good things would come to me. This belief all changed when I found myself suffering and broken with a workplace injury. Fibromyalgia was the label, yet it was so much more. Just like the early days of Chronic Fatigue, Fibromyalgia is sometimes a diagnosis given when they do not honestly know what is wrong.

I was broken, bruised, overworked, overwhelmed, and traumatized. In the space of a short few months I lost my reputation, my 'status' as the reliable go-to-girl I had carefully groomed. So much so that I had been headhunted to rebuild the culture of a team of rebellious competitive bullies.

It wasn't so much the stress of being the 'new girl' in an environment of workplace competition and jealously preventing what could have otherwise been a dynamic and robustly resourceful team. When things began to fall from my hands indiscriminately, and the throbbing and inflammation in my wrists halted any stress-relieving extracurricular activity I enjoyed, I realized that a shift was about to happen.

I know that this story is supposed to be inspirational. At this point, you can see that all we have our problems and trauma. Indeed, at that time all life seemed to offer was problems and trauma. It wasn't until quite sometime later that epiphanies showed how problematic this lifestyle was. When, at its worst, I was unable to feed or clothe myself comfortably. I struggled to wash my hair. Embarrassed and ashamed, I suffered.

So let's fast forward to eight years later. Insurance payments had ceased. Court proceedings finalized and all appeals failed. The company began to offer redundancy payouts. Despite providing it to all of my fully functional colleagues, they chose to deny mine. It was during my processing of this decision that the revelations truly hit.

The payout would have cleared all my debts and provided an opportunity to rebuild my life. Their refusal effectively rendered me homeless. While this may be shocking to you, I now know it was perhaps the most potent catalyst of self-love I have ever experienced. For maybe the first time in my life, I had no option but to reach out. I had to ask others for help.

A lifetime I had spent believing hard work and doing my best would lead to a good life. The whole time I also felt that I was in it alone. If it had to be, it was up to me.

In trying to do everything on my own, I felt that nobody was supporting or loving me. When I had to leave my apartment and sell all that I owned, I did what I'd never done before. I reached out to people I barely knew to ask for support, and they surprisingly held me.

To this day, I have always had a bed to sleep in, food in my mouth and clean clothes. In asking for help, I gave others the opportunity to support and love me. The whole eight years I suffered, I suffered alone. With loving support, even though I couldn't afford to pay rent, I decided to use my gifts of dance to help those who didn't feel the support I had received. And so, I started a dance by donation class directing funds to a local women's shelter.

My experience taught me that, homelessness is directly impacted by the absence of love. Interestingly, while I may not be wealthy, my fibromyalgia is almost entirely gone.

Breaking Free
By Leah Recor

Who I am today didn't begin the day I was born. Nor did it start the day my mother was born, nor her mother. I am an unconscious co-creation of the beliefs and expectations of our culture which began the day civilization was born. However, what I chose to be moving forward, that is my creation. Who I am today, each day, is a result of my breaking free and waking up. And I will never go back.

As a woman in the United States, I did as my mother taught me, and inevitably, as she was instructed. Through words and modeled behavior, I learned to be kind, quiet, and in-service of others and trusting others would do the right thing if I did not assert myself.

My mother passed away when I was 21. I realized, while she made every effort to serve and protect me, she left me paralyzed to defend myself. I repeated her patterns and became a victim of my life, just as she energetically modeled.

For the next 20 years, I would find life happening to me. Both in good and bad ways, somehow I would always find myself at the whim of this perceived master of my destiny. When I experienced assault, infertility, a devastating divorce and continued disappointment in the culture of man, it was always with the understanding I would have to endure these experiences, powerlessly.

I kept grasping at my perception of control only to find it being stripped away repeatedly. The misconception that I gained power by controlling situations was exhausting and created patterns of hopelessness and anxiety. My life wasn't meant to be this way. I had so much more to give. There was more to me than being a single mom, relying on government assistance with a low paying job which caused me to be away from my kids regularly.

Raising two little girls who were already modeling my energy of dissatisfaction, victimization, irrationality, and desperation, I couldn't imagine allowing them to repeat the patterns of my life, my mother's life, and all the women that came before us. I realized I would need to trust the Universe because trying to control it was not working. I just let go—a giant trust fall with the Universe.

It was in allowing the hard times in life to be lessons and guidance that I began to exert real control over my life. I became a master of my emotions, always checking in with my sadness, fear, and anger seeing where or who those feelings were coming from and managing them while also modeling my new emotional awareness for my kids.

I began consciously creating my life. I was attracting healthier friendships into my life, and unhealthy relationships were fading away. I was building businesses that were in service to others and manifesting everyday signs into my life that kept my thoughts positive and lovingly prepared. The best part was that I taught my daughters their power. I saw an enormous shift in their self-esteem, peer dynamics, and belief in the Universe to support them in consciously creating their path and finding their purpose.

We may be women who have energetically accepted the path that had been laid by the women that came before us, but we are also powerful creators. We need only awaken to the incredible forces that are at play in our existence. Let us all help each other awaken; then let us consciously co-create an incredible new reality.

Conquering Day-to-Day Anxiety
By Anna Pitchouguina

I am easily swayed off my path. Sometimes, when I am in my right element, I see the journey I create. I can help others, and I acknowledge my achievements and self-worth. Albeit, other times I stray, and my mind, my feet, my heart, my ego, and my soul all wander off into different directions, and I find myself very anxious.

Sometimes I can become so disenfranchised that I forget who I truly am and I feel lost. I lend myself to becoming all that I am not. I meander through the corridors of my past and fear that my future will be shrouded with dark tunnels. I can be existent anywhere and everywhere and in the magnitude of infinite possibilities, I find myself stuck in the space of fear. It is at those times that the shadows consume me and it all starts to flood in: trauma, judgment, guilt, and shame.

Long ago, the damage was done. I want to say I'm healed, but then something happens; a trigger, a memory, and down the rabbit hole I go, left to battle my psyche, the phantoms of my past. I lose the focus, stillness, and peace that I fought so fiercely to create and I give up the steering wheel of the aircraft of which I am supposed to be the pilot. I resign my sovereignty to external forces and become a product of my surroundings and the projections of what others think I am.

I indulge in a victim identity to which I am the perpetrator; I suffer, and I cause suffering. I no longer hold the position of the architect over my reality, and my very being becomes directed and dictated by all that I am not. This downward spiral happens so seamlessly that I am not aware of its occurrence. It takes time for me to realize that I am struggling with myself, or rather with a false sense of self. When understanding comes, I remember to breathe. I pause. I slowly and gently lead myself back to my path. If I was able to get through the traumatic events that have caused this present anxiety, then I am just as capable of overcoming this residual effect.

Throughout it all, I remain grateful for I know how to bounce back and how to shape and manifest the reality of myself that truly reflects my essence; one without falsehoods and struggle, one without the attachment and projection of who I was along my past events and my present and future anxieties associated with those experiences. I empower myself to regain control and stay firmly grounded in the truth of all that I am, without giving myself a hard time for having deviated from myself in the first place.

I acknowledge that I will have to repeat this process as a daily ritual. My state of stillness is transient, yet so too is the anxiety. I am where I need to be, anxious and all. Even when I am not where I need to be, physically, emotionally, and spiritually, I am still where I need to be, for I am always best placed to come back to me.

Bounce House Adventure
By Katie Smock

I remember the day my victorious, entrepreneurial spirit kicked into full throttle mode. You know that exciting day that you tell yourself you are going to make something happen, and hopefully, you make it big! My friend and I decided to go on an adventure and purchase bounce houses that we could rent out. Our first gig was at a parade. We set up in a parking lot for free. We had no experience, no training, just an audience, and a naive hope that this would magically work.

The beginning of this task was to merely unload and unroll the large vinyl unit and attach a blower. A blower is a device you use to pump air into the bounce house. Seems super simple, right? We attached a blower to inflate the bounce house and watched as our dream started to fill with hope and excitement. Larger and larger it expanded as it rose in the air and stretched out to what seemed to be in the direction of full capacity. Something happened though—the massive bounce house stopped inflating. It looked like a sad, soggy noodle. As I stated before, we had no training, so now began the guessing game. What could have been wrong?

We thought maybe we could push it or prod it to help it up. So, we tried that, and it still flopped over like a sad child that was just told, "No." Next, we thought that maybe if we got inside the bounce house and pushed things around in it, it would pop up. That had to work, right? Nope, it still didn't happen. At this point, we decided to think outside the box. What if we needed another blower to fix the problem? Maybe it just needed more power. Maybe the power we were using somehow wasn't cutting it. I grabbed another blower and generator to see if doubling the airflow would do the trick. At this point, the parade was going to start soon. We had an audience that wanted to bounce in this new business venture, and there was no bouncing happening. The blower was added, and the generator was turned on. I took a step back, within myself I thought, "This is going to work, this is going to happen. I will make it happen."

Well, it didn't. "How could this be happening?" I thought. My next thought was that maybe there was a rip somewhere that I wasn't seeing. Something had to be wrong with this bounce house for it not to be working. My search continued to look for this hypothetical rip. I couldn't find a tear. At this moment I got angry, sad, upset, and ready to cry, but mostly just angry. I was not willing to give up. I was prepared to dig in and be unrelenting. After all, making this business adventure a reality was my hope and dream. I took a deep breath and looked over every square inch of the bounce house. Then finally, a simple solution was found! There was a two-foot wide zipper that was open. I screamed with joy, closed the zipper, and that fixed the problem. The bounce house fully inflated and everyone had a good time.

That is how life goes. For our dreams to become a reality, we have to push and prod, add extra oomph and power, and check for rips. Ultimately, we need to realize that if we would only zip up the big hole that is letting out our air, things come together and we rise.

The Battle I Chose Not to Fight
By Courtney Beeren

When I was a little girl, I would to sit and watch my mother put her makeup on before she would go out. I would sit on the edge of the bed and look at my mum, feeling love for her. She was the most beautiful woman in the world. I felt lucky to have her.

I was four when my parents separated. I experienced the first traumatic moment of my short life when my mum dragged me out of the family home, kicking and screaming while Dad could do nothing. It still sends chills down my spine.

From that day, I didn't see Mum as beautiful anymore. How could she do this to me? I didn't want to move to a new house with another man. I wanted Dad. I wanted to feel safe and loved. Instead, I felt like I was being packed up like one of my mother's handbags.

For years after that, I struggled with trust, love, and confidence. I hid myself every chance I got. I felt unimportant, and my mother and friends treated me that way. I was the weirdo. I talked to myself, had imaginary friends, and wanted to live in a Disney movie where someone would come and rescue me. They never did.

As I grew into a teenager, life became more complicated. The usual side-effects kicked in like hormones (crushes on boys and such), but I had other things that concerned me. While my mother and stepfather drank, fought and struggled with their demons, I took care of my younger brothers. I didn't go out with friends. That would mean asking Mum for a ride, or not being home to make dinner or put my brothers to bed. And with that came the emotional manipulation from Mum. That was the worst part. The woman who was supposed to look after me, guide me, show me how to be an adult, expected that from me instead.

This hold she had over me continued for many more years until I realized this relationship did not serve me, it didn't bring me any joy or feelings of love. There was nothing but a sick feeling in the pit of my stomach every time I saw her number on the caller ID. I felt the dread of hearing the sound of her voice and conforming to what she wanted me to be.

I haven't spoken to my mother in six years. I finally had had enough. I couldn't see why I was punishing myself to try and help someone who didn't want to help themselves— someone who continually played the victim.

I realized that I wasn't supposed to have a mother who was also my best friend. I wasn't supposed to be able to ask for her advice, or even introduce her to my husband. That's not the mother I was destined to have, and that's okay. The most potent decision I made was accepting that our relationship was meant to challenge us. We were not meant to have a happy ending. I'm proud of the decision I made. It made me who I am today. That was part of my story, and I can choose how the story ends.

I see my emotional bruises and wounds, and I love them. I'm thankful for them. They taught me compassion, forgiveness, and honesty.

So thank you, Mum, and I forgive you. And you did teach me, just not in the way I expected.

The Power of Choice
By Kat Saraswati

For most of my life, I have been relatively reclusive. I remember hiding from my family and the world. Thinking no one understood or cared about the shame and pain I was feeling, I kept everyone (even my husband) at a distance. I had the outward appearance of being strong and not letting anyone know that I was always waiting for the other shoe to drop. I smiled on the outside while a raging beast lay hidden inside, waiting to release its wrath on those closest to me. I worked with psychologists and psychiatrists over the years hoping to find relief from the pain and shame of being sexually abused as a child. I always wondered why my grandfather chose me as his victim. What did I do to deserve this abuse? I never trusted or believed that I deserved to be loved. I believed enjoying sex was somehow wrong. I was dirty and not deserving of love. I was damaged, and believed that my husband would eventually find a better sexual partner to fulfill his needs.

For years, my husband and I struggled to find a sustaining sense of peace with my obsessive behavior. The more he tried to show me how much he cared and the beauty that he saw inside of me, the more I fought to see anything but ugliness. My relationship with my husband and my professional career was crumbling from all the emotional strain I had created. I was ready to throw in the towel and give up on everything, everyone, and life itself. Then I met Dr. Nataleah Rose Schotte. It was the exact turning point in my life. I spent months working with Dr. Nataleah to release the pain and tap into my real potential. I discovered a strength and beauty inside. However, universal law dictates there is always darkness where there is light. In acknowledging that the divine was within, I had to accept responsibility for the sorrow and destruction I created. I was the only one responsible for the life, the reality I had created. I had to stare into the mirror and see the beauty and imperfections.

I was at a point of transformation. A transformation is a conscious act which requires continuous progress toward something new. I had reached a crossroads in my life where I could choose to return to what was comfortable or take on the challenge to become the greatness I genuinely am. I was struggling with the possibility of being free of the self-judgment and self-destruction. This unfamiliar territory caused me to feel lost. As I ventured through unchartered waters, I sought solace and refuge in the resonance of my gongs and Himalayan Singing Bowls and the teaching of the Bön. I was unconsciously creating a sanctuary where I would not have to choose—a sanctuary where I suspended all possibility of growth.

Spirituality has its place in personal growth, however, I was fortunate to recognize that I was using my spiritual practice to keep myself in a state of unconscious bliss and refusing to allow the greatness of me to unfold. I wanted to be the architect of my life, so I choose to let go of people and beliefs that I had once used to define me. I began to perceive and receive a reality different from anything I had created in the past. I am grateful to those who have assisted me to see I deserve more. So, while I may falter from time to time, it is an exhilarating feeling to know that I will always be greater tomorrow than I am today. It's my *choice*.

The Anchor
By Ann Agueli

Scheduled for Thursday morning at 7:00 a.m. was my procedure, and I felt utterly alone. The feeling of going through this procedure without a life partner wanted to take me down. It didn't matter I had female support; the lack of support from a man is what held my focus.

The Unthinkable Happens: Why God Why?

At the corner of, "Why God Why?" and the intersection of "I Feel So Alone," the unthinkable happened; I had to take my daughter to the emergency clinic where she fainted in my arms after receiving an injection for an allergic reaction. It was just 48 hours before my procedure.

All my life, I've had a panic disorder, and I couldn't fathom how these circumstances were orchestrating in my life. All I could focus on was my daughter, even though she was okay now. I thought to myself, 'I'm single; who will take care of her if something happened to me?' Yes, of course, she had a father who loved her, but he wasn't 'mommy;' no one was. It didn't matter she was a teen; I'd always be 'mommy' (in my heart anyway). I just wanted to be in control, and when I realized I wasn't, I panicked.

On Being Quiet

I awoke at 4:00 a.m. that Thursday, fully intending to cancel my procedure. I was *not* going under anesthesia and risking something happening. As I sat quietly on my bed, I sent out a text to my male best-friend (at the time) who was always there for me in tough times. He didn't respond; my panic escalated. I remember sitting on the edge of my bed, closing my eyes, praying to God, asking Him what to do.

The Anchor

I distinctly remember, as if it were today, in the stillness of the morning, I heard God say, "Do you think I would let anything happen to you?" I felt a presence so real in my chest, connecting me to Him like an anchor. I had a vision in my mind's eye. I saw God's hand lifting me as I was hanging on to the end of dark and ugly roots, clinging to them for dear life. I saw God gently shake me off the end of those roots I so desperately wanted to hang on to as I landed on empty, barren land.

Breathlessly, I asked, "Why are you leaving me here all alone without my old story. You've left me here on the barren ground." To which I heard the reply, "I've left you on fertile soil, a new clearing and a new place to sow."

I understood from that moment on; God was my constant. He was my all and my everything. I knew I could depend on Him. God hand-picked my old story of 'being alone/of not being good enough' right out of me; showing me He was the one on which I could depend—always. I accepted God's invitation to plant rows of faith, mounds of trust, and sow seeds of surrender as I went forward with the procedure. I allowed God to fertilize my new crops with His All-Knowing, unconditional love.

A New Story: Rewrite the Script

When the story and that human vulnerability returns, I can return to this memory; I can also choose. I can choose to rewrite the script of 'being alone/not being good enough' to one of 'God fully and wholly supports me.' Praise and glory to God. I can choose to believe God is depositing me on fertile soil. The longer we hold onto an old story God is trying to remove, the longer we delay the new crop God has in store.

Go ahead and plant new seeds.

Angel Wings Tatoo
By Joi Hayes

"Mom, can I get a tattoo of the angel wings on my elbow?" That sentence from my daughter evokes so many emotions in my heart. March 13, 2017, I received a phone call. "Your daughter has been in an accident, please come quickly." Leaving a full shopping cart, I rush to the car with tears streaming down my face. I don't remember the drive to the hospital.

So many people are talking to me, around me and all the hospital noises are overwhelming. I only want to see my daughter's face. All the air leaves the room as I see tubes, road rash, blood and marker on her face and body; head shaved, limp, a lifeless body and the only thing I can think is, 'Will her eyes open again?'

I am helpless; time has stopped. I don't know how to restart my heart. I don't know anything, but I have to breathe. I ask the nurse if I can touch her. May I please wash the blood off her hands and face?

Prayers are coming hard and fast as I gently wash my daughter, the child I held in my arms 22 years ago. I ask for strength; I pray for angels. I think, 'What will I do if I lose her?

Where will I get my strength?' I had strayed from asking my angels for help. Yes, I have angels. They have protected me many times, yet I lost touch in the last ten years. Would they come to me when I needed them the most? I asked, and I received. Tears ran down my face; I felt as if the room was filled with loving healing angels and they were embracing us. I know I can get through this, I know I will be guided. They will be here 24/7 even when I can't be.

Every day is a new journey with new complications. Every night I cry, journal the day and read the notes from when I was not there. I am grateful for friends and family who brought food, came at 2:30 in the morning on sleepless nights or sat with her when I could not be there. I am grateful for miracle after miracle, being walked through this journey, never feeling alone.

My beautiful daughter would undergo five surgeries, including taking a piece of her skull out to let the brain swell, multiple setbacks and finally rehab. Surgery on September, 11, 2017 put the piece of skull back into her head. A whirlwind six months ending on September 13, 2017 (yes, just six months after the accident she walked out of the hospital), and one month later, she went back to work. Short hair and a scar are the only telltale signs of the life-changing ordeal that both broke me and then built me back up.

Here we sit today, her with a sassy look and her short red hair; me, a Mom filled with love and gratitude and wondering where I will put my angel wing tattoo.

The Ring
By TC Gavlin

One morning as I walked my dog Stella and communed with the trees, I focused and vibrated the mantra, "Separation is an illusion; I am whole and complete." As a woman in my 50's, I'd begun a daily meditation practice with the desire to make peace with the past, to quiet my mind, and to heal from broken relationships.

Toward the end of the mile-loop, I watched a man dismount his bike in the road. Approaching him, I asked if he'd lost something. He looked up from the street and responded, "My wedding ring." I could relate to losing something special, and offered to help, tying Stella's leash to a neighbor's tree.

With a flick of his wrist, he demonstrated how the ring slipped off his finger. Now I used logic, by considering the placement of his hand and the pitch of the road to reason its likely path. It was possible the ring rolled to the left side, heading north. We split up, looking in separate areas.

Twenty minutes passed, he thanked me and shrugged saying that it was wishful thinking to find it. He mounted his road bike, apparently giving up. I suggested we continue to focus on the possibility of finding the ring. I introduced myself and resumed my quest.

After learning his name, I asked Jon about his platinum wedding band. My ego wanted to find it, to be helpful, to be right, and to save the day. I soon came to realize I was not present or open to intuition.

I recalled how an intuitive does not process with an analytical mind, but rather utilizes other methods to access a greater intelligence that is within and around everything. I sensed the ring at some distance.

I began to quiet thought by centering on my heart, to seek direction and allow guidance about the ring's course. It is not lost, and I am not separate from it. I felt a pull to raise my gaze and broaden my vision to the center of the road. I had focused in too tight of an area, in my will and analysis.

Gazing in a new direction, I visualized and sensed the soft sheen of a platinum ring. I walked to the opposite side of the street and began again, walking along the curb, gently spreading leaves with my foot. Time passed, doubt sunk in and I stopped. What if this is wrong? I paused and was still until assurance came through to keep moving forward.

Continuing to a gutter drain, I briefly wondered if it had fallen through the grate. I then stopped to focus and center once more. With renewed clarity, I opened my eyes and felt guided to look ahead, believing the ring was near. At about 12 feet, I spotted a glint of light, partially hidden in dark leaves. Heart pounding, I moved toward the ring. It was shining softly, resting in the place where it had rolled. I picked it up, excited to hold it. It felt heavy in my palm from the platinum and the promises. I briefly slipped it on my right index finger and whispered thank you, feeling blessed.

I called to Jon who was searching further up the street, who had never left, and walked quickly to him, feeling both grateful and elated. Jon yelled, "You found it? You are awesome!" I handed it to him and once on his finger, he thanked me for not giving up and for finding his ring.

As I approached home with Stella, Jon biked up to thank me one more time and it occurred to me that now we are connected. I am part of his story and he is part of mine.

Dyslexia Is My Superpower
By Gibby Booth Jasper

A freaking positive? My business coach must be joking, but who would joke about that? Laura had just told me my cancer was a good thing. Okay, well, to be honest, I'm talking about my dyslexia, but it felt that extreme to me. Dyslexia made me think from the age of five that I was stupid. It made me deathly nervous talking to people because I was never sure what would come out of my mouth, and for a good reason. In 4th grade, during a presentation on the ocean, I said octopuses have eight testicles. And then in 6th grade helping with a car-pooling arrangement, I told the class that Sarah's mother had an STD, instead of an SUV. Sarah never really talked to me again after that. I was convinced that I had become a successful entrepreneur despite my dyslexia not because of it—full stop, end of story. Laura kept insisting that it was a positive attribute. However, that was a load of crap. Not being dyslexic herself, she couldn't understand.

Frustratingly, when I woke up the next morning the thought was still there. It was like having an angel and a devil on each of my shoulders. They kept bickering back and forth, debating whether dyslexia was a positive or not. I couldn't understand why this was happening. Hadn't I already determined it wasn't a positive? Weren't my life's struggles with all the embarrassment and shame proof of that?

As the day continued, their back and forth arguing got louder and louder. They didn't care if I was in the shower, driving to work, or with a client, they just kept at it. I had finally had it that evening while chopping carrots for dinner. "Enough!" I yelled, throwing my arms into the air sending carrots flying and my dog running for cover. "Fine, I'll look into it!" I bellowed. 'Great,' I thought, 'now I'm talking to myself.' I put down the knife, collected the escaped veggies and googled, 'positives of dyslexia.'

I'm not sure what I expected, but nothing of real substance. I stumbled across a website called Nessy.com and started reading their list of dyslexia strengths and couldn't believe it. There they were—the parts of my character that I valued the most: being a visual thinker, able to see the bigger picture, and thinking outside the box, to name a few. It was in that moment that it struck me: I had only been looking at my dyslexia through a negative lens, not even acknowledging there was an upside. The truth is, dyslexia was both. Yes, it made reading and writing challenging and made me say the wrong word, but it also made me a successful entrepreneur and gave me the ability to see things from a different angle, which I valued so highly.

I want to say that after that moment, my life changed in an instant and I never had any problems with my dyslexia again. But that's not entirely true! What I can honestly say is that it was a huge turning point that set me on a journey to discover more about dyslexia and ultimately about myself. This turning point led me to go from hating my dyslexia to respecting it, to now loving and fully embracing it. I can see the humor in the moments where I say things like intimate instead of immediate. What I came to realize is that my dyslexia got me where I am today, and it's why I proudly call it my superpower and wear it as a badge of honor.

The Heart Asks No Questions First
By Saxon Brazier

Growing up in a home with a violent, twisted schizophrenic brother and a transient mother, I found my formative years confusing. Other children made fun of me for my long red hair and my strange name (Saxon Stardust). Why they did this was a mystery to me. I was just a little sensitive having a heartbeat much like everyone else.

It was later on when I discovered adult dynamics where the parents of other children would speak in hateful ways. They were afraid of my mother's gypsy ways with her single mother status, and Stevie Nicks' looks which made the conservative mothers hold fast to their husbands, perceiving a threat. That created a trickle-down effect which passed onto their children. I was ostracized as a result by my community. This experience has been my greatest gift. To know I'm different and be okay with it has taught me more than the many diplomas and degrees I have been so eager to achieve.

I do carry the archetype of the overachiever as I feel I have something to prove to myself. I was born into a family which generated addiction and mental health issues with great intergenerational trauma. However, it does not mean that I can't grow into my brand of Heroine. And so I thrive, and I rise. Every year I'm not sticking a needle into my veins to reinvent myself, I am growing in love—cast iron self-belief with diamond and platinum spirals cascading around my heart. My heart is my crowning jewel.

Sexually abused, a victim of rape, abandonment and narcissistic relationships grow my soul's mission to always lead with the heart at all costs, no matter what. I know a certain resilience and fundamental truth that no man can ever take away from me. I share it with every soul whom I am lucky enough to come into contact.

You can let your experience be the bedrock of failure. You almost have a free get out of jail card to not rise, to stay in your comfort zone and not re-trigger your trauma story or PTSD. You can also choose to wake up every morning with the greatest compassion for yourself. You know you are a survivor. You are unbreakable, unshakable and share that gift with the world. Show the world that they can do the same.

The heart forgives over and over and over again. It's your ego you want to get on your side. It's your ego that you need to become teammates. And once you do, you will rise to heights within yourself that never cease to ascend.

Annie
By Dana Parker

Annie was smart, good-looking, friendly, compassionate and kind. She always had a smile and a sneaky sense of humor that would make you laugh. One blessed day she turned up at my Tango class, and within a short time, I loved her.

It wasn't just a dance teacher-student relationship. A professional dancer for Alvin Alley in New York in her late teens, she was the only Australian dancer back when they had a rainbow-colored cast. It had been my high school dream to dance for Alvin Alley. So, you can imagine my delight when she arrived.

Of course, she had fallen in love, gotten pregnant and ended her dance career in her 20s, as many a woman has want of doing. In class, she was eager and enthusiastic for the reconnect.

When I met Annie, I felt an immediate affinity with her. I used to say just knowing she existed made me feel better. It was my first sense that there was a Soul Tribe out there. And it was mutual. At the end of my class, she would say, "Thank you for giving me back my dance. More people need to know about you!" Words I would laugh off with humility.

In 2014, a stream of extraordinary events led to a breakdown into mental illness, a struggle Annie lost along with her life. At the time, the Tango community was devastated. Her loss came as a huge shock.

For me, the situation became a catalyst. I had always seen Annie as a role model. Like many women, she had suffered a tragic life behind closed doors. Very few people knew of her internal struggles. She presented as a high achieving woman, having it "all together."

When she left, she took a piece of me with her. I saw the similarities between us acutely and had to acknowledge the internal struggles within me.

Before she passed, we sat together to write a list of things we would do when she recovered. She had been re-diagnosed with Post Traumatic Stress Disorder, a legacy from her early life. She wanted to make a difference for women in similar situations.

While not well known, a workplace injury in 2008 effectively rendered me unable to use my arms properly. A brain injury, coupled with autonomic nervous system dysfunction and autoimmune disease, it had me declared unfit to work. Recovery was painful, a journey of suffering that I kept primarily hidden. With Annie's encouragement, I began to attend lectures on modern neuroscience. As my number one fan, she attended every single one with me.

It was not long after Annie died that I began to ask new questions. Why are we trying so hard to be all things for all people? Why can't we be okay with ourselves?

And so, I made a decision. It was time to step out of the closet; time to be seen, heard and known. If nothing else, I would be free of compromise to be 'all of that' for other people's sensibilities. If it had to be, it was up to me. So, I pulled up my big girl pants and stepped into myself.

"More people need to know about you."

Months later, I started my first Movement Energetics class and stepped into my spiritual awakening. Now, I specialize in supporting women as they explore their spiritual awakening. I witness them stepping in and expressing their unique gifts in the world. I travel the world doing this and Annie would love what I do.

And it began the Sacred Rose Awakening.

The Promise
By Kyra Schaefer

There is a part of me that is hesitant to write this story, to have it in black and white for all to see. I firmly believe that once a story is told, the healing begins. I have mentioned this story to many people over the years, often to help others see they aren't alone. Other times, to help me heal this story and have it released, I tell it here to help those who may have suffered from domestic violence. I was once engaged to a man who didn't know himself. He was unable to get out from under his addictions and his hostile ways.

One night, in particular, he got the better of me. He punched me, knocked me down and kicked me in the head while I lay on my front porch. He returned to the kitchen to find more beer and in my almost unconscious state realized I was trying to kill myself, and I was going to use him to do it. I was incredibly unhappy, also addicted and hostile. I was lost. When I became more conscious, I took that moment to talk to God. I said, "Dear God, if you let me live I will spend my life serving you; otherwise, let him kill me." A burst of energy flowed through me. I sat up and walked into the house where he was opening another beer. I grabbed the phone and dialed 911.

"Dispatch, what's your emergency?" a confident voice came over the phone.

"We are having a domestic disturbance," I stated.

Then my ex-fiancé walked over and repeated me, "A domestic disturbance, a domestic disturbance?" and head-butted me in the face while I was on the phone. I couldn't feel anything. All I could feel was the love of God moving through my body, mind, and spirit.

"Ma'am, are you still on the line?" The dispatcher asked.

"Yes, he head-butted me," I responded.

"Stay on the line, help is on the way," the dispatcher reassured.

My ex left, he was picked up by the police at a friend's house and I wouldn't see him again until the court date, which later ruled in my favor.

As I look back on that night 20 years later, I can say with certainty without this experience I wouldn't have taken the journey I did.

I have devoted my life to being of service and to help others to the best of my ability. I became a Reiki Practitioner, a Clinical Hypnosis Instructor and now I own a publishing company to help healers give voice to their passion. I have helped thousands of people. I kept and continued to follow the promise I made on that chilly night so many years ago.

Soul's Calling
By Dina F. Gilmore

I believe my entire life has been a spiritual journey and thankfully so. I overcame childhood abuse, being disowned by my family and homeless after coming out as gay in my teens, dropping out of college and leaving my art dreams behind. I felt utterly alone and like a massive disappointment, so I attempted suicide at twenty-two. I survived that day because there was an unknown higher purpose and there was no medical explanation as to how I survived. I was saved by God, a higher power, creator, source—however you believe is beautiful. I put myself in counseling, received hypnotherapy, massage therapy, learned meditation, attended spiritual retreats, which all led me to become a healer for other people. I am clear that becoming a Licensed Massage Therapist in 2000 was the big stepping stone to a grander path of healing.

I attribute a vast majority of my healing through Shamanism and the ancient art of the Shamanic Journey, which can be compared to a meditative type state. I never resonated with a specific religion even though my family comes from devout Southern Baptist roots. My heart and soul thirsted for more consciousness, more love, acceptance, and a peaceful way. I went to my first book club group in 2004, and the subject was on a book called "Soul Retrieval" by Sandra Ingerman. This early introduction into

Shamanism sang to my soul and unleashed my spirit that ultimately gave me the lost connection to my Cherokee heritage. I finally felt like I found a home, community, and happily stepped into my purpose. I continued to study for the next five years from basic to advanced classes and received my right of passage in 2009 from Spirit Moon Community as a Shamanic Practitioner. I have continued my teachings from Shamans in New Mexico, Nepal, and Peru to keep learning from other healers.

Another big stepping stone was when I visited Colorado in December 2011, and the mountains beckoned to my soul. I knew my life in Texas was complete and I craved change. I wanted to live in a more progressive and accepting environment, so five months later I boldly packed up my entire life and relocated to Denver. The best decision I ever made was taking this brave new action, returning to college, and living my life for me! Going back to college has provided a sense of fulfillment in finishing what I started in 1989, gave me a newfound love in photography, and expanded creative outlets for my writing. My soul called me to the mountains, so I could find myself, bring my biggest dreams into reality, and leave a loving impact on the world.

My most recent stepping stone was listening to messages that inspired me to create my spiritual business, "Mobile Shaman," and experience more of the world. The vision behind my company is traveling to different cities leading Shamanic Journey Circles. I teach classes, offer retreats to build community, connection, and empower every life I am blessed to encounter. I now have two spiritually gifted souls, Jai and Tree, who have joined beside me for leading events. My journey circles have morphed into

Shamanic Sound Journeys and collaborations with these lovely women playing their Gongs, Crystal and Tibetan Metal Bowls. By changing from one to three aligned together, we have been able to offer more profound state journeys by incorporating Sound Healing. One of my favorite sayings is, 'The most wounded souls make the best healers,' and I answer that call proudly where healing is needed. Love, healing, and impactful journeys to you. Blessings!

Finding the Good in Chaos
By Tosha Fields

I was born with a genetic disease called Sickle Cell Anemia. Most people I encounter don't know what that is, so let me explain. This disease causes the red blood cells in the body to become malformed in the shape of a sickle. The red blood cells in our body carry oxygen and nutrients. My body is deprived of the oxygen that is needed to be healthy and because the cells are no longer round in shape, thereby cutting the veins, trying to pass causing severe pain throughout the body.

Now that we have the basics of how the disease process functions, I can tell you about being a kid in pain. None of the many doctors my mother took me to were able to tell us why this was happening. It was incredibly frustrating. I learned later that I was in a pain crisis and they didn't know how to treat me. All I could do was lay there in pain and wait for it to be over. My mother felt helpless, and that caused her great sadness, to watch her baby in pain.

As I got older and started school, my pain crisis made it difficult to make friends. The children would call me names. I was a loner, and that mindset has continued to be true all of my life. As an adult, maintaining relationships was a struggle. There was still a part of a broken-hearted child that wanted to be accepted and be considered society's standard of normal. Being in and out of hospitals didn't leave me time to build those bonds with others. I knew that I was studious and that is where I spent my time. As I became an adult, I now realize I had enough skills to be among others, but it could have been better.

After my mother passed away, I made mistakes and I was and had always been an emotional person. I stuffed all those emotions down because I was harshly judged and became a person that wouldn't show any feelings to anyone. Now that I'm much older, I'm still learning how to now show those emotions without the fear and anxiety of being hurt. I know that I must and can do so, but only with God's help. Thus far, dealing with this chaos in my mind has been a challenge, but it is worth it to be the woman that I want and need to be. I've been there and fought for everyone else, and now it's time to fight for my life and have the things I desire and more.

I am continually told who I am and my faults and where improvements can be made in life. It's not all from a place of malice, some in love. Some are observations and perceptions to give me insight into how the world views me because I can't change what I don't know and recognize as something to take to God. I'm so turned around and confused about who I am and who I need to be, what's right and what's wrong. I have to consult God in the middle of this chaos, to hear the quiet in the storm.

This journey has been and will be the hardest and most fulfilling journey to date, but I am looking forward to victory and the pleasure of knowing myself the way God knows me. I leave room for continual growth spiritually, socially, physically, emotionally, and mentally. We all can fight to be better people even though the challenges life can bring our way are difficult. Find the peace, comfort, and strength amongst the chaos in our life.

New York State of Body, Mind, Spirit
By Chelley Canales

It's Wednesday morning and I've had this Southampton beach mostly to myself for hours. The water is cold, and I'm too scared to submerge myself in the Atlantic fully. Mother Nature has other plans and aggressively knocks me on my butt with an enormous wave, as if to say, "If you don't jump in and go with the flow, life's gonna force you in and you won't have a choice on how it happens." Thank you. Noted.

When one door closes, another one opens, but it's hell in the hallways. This is the "be still" portion of my time in the hallway, the one I intentionally threw myself into, and I'm constantly reminding myself to be present. Remembering this, I set my timer for ten minutes to tune in and meditate, a reprieve from the mental noise. This stillness is challenging for me. Having control of situations has always given me a sense of security but rarely produced the desired results. I can't force the answers to come, so I'm sitting with myself, awaiting the next step. I stave off the panic of not having a job lined up starting next month. I must remember I chose this. I'm still glad I did.

I imagined this trip to NYC for a few reasons, one being closure. It's been almost five years since I've moved away and it wasn't until now that I wanted to come back. There was too much pain around it. I suspect that after all these years of processing my journey it finally occurred to me that there were pieces of myself left behind. If I wanted to move forward to the next chapter of my life, I had to look back first, so I decided to visit the landmarks of my old life and reclaim the missing pieces.

How does one do that, Chell? Great question. It has to do with ritual: visiting the location, letting the emotions arise, and then clearing them. I stop and fully remember the situation but bring love and compassion to myself, a reminder that I did the best I could at the time. I then send love and forgiveness to anyone associated with the memory that I perceived as being hurtful to me. I thank the Universe for the lessons, take the valuable information with me and leave the hurt behind. It no longer serves me, and it is forever released back into the ether.

My walking tour of Astoria yesterday gave me the first taste of this unique form of emotional clearing. A million memories, both little and life-changing, were revisited, felt, held and released. I replaced the remnants of sadness that remained with a new, joyful memory, grateful that those experiences helped turn me into the much wiser, and whole woman I am today. I'll revisit the Manhattan and Brooklyn chapters of my life in the coming days, but for now, I'm enjoying these thoughts rolling in as I watch the Atlantic waves roll out.

Whether we realize it or not, we carry around the energy of old wounds, even if we hardly think of them anymore or feel confident we've already dealt with them. The more I reconnect with my spirituality, the more I realize how important it is to reflect and to clear this old energy. It's stagnant and heavy and takes up space in my body, mind, and spirit that should be used for creating something new.

As I sit on this beach, I am so grateful for the opportunity to have a fresh start any time I choose. I allow the waves to crash over my body, wiping my slate clean.

The Choice
By Julianna Nelson

I didn't realize that I was surviving—until I was thriving. Have you ever had a nagging feeling that there is something more? That just beyond your reach—physically, mentally, emotionally—there is more fulfillment, more love, and more joy?

Life was good. My job was fine; my kids were fine, my income was fine—nothing to complain about, yet, nothing to celebrate. Everything was…fine.

And then things weren't fine. On December 19th, 2015, my two daughters and I (and so many others who were close to him - became the "survivors" of suicide. I use the word survivor because suicide so deeply traumatizes you, it is as if you are a part of it.

'Fine' did not exist anymore. Some days it took every ounce of strength to survive. My reaction to my ex-husband's suicide was to question every single aspect of my life, my role as mother, wife, daughter, friend, and employee. What did it mean? How had I contributed? How did I not see? What could I have done? What do I do now? How do I keep my children safe? How do I heal their hurt that is *so* profound?

Spinning, spinning, spinning. Further and further and further away from thriving. Am I even surviving? Until one day, the free-fall from my past life ended, and I landed on solid ground. And I became silent. And for the first time in my life, I listened. I listened to myself. I listened to the nagging feeling that maybe, just maybe, life could be more than 'fine.'

I began the gentle journey into the unknown land of me. I explored who I was 'before', because now there was 'before' and 'after' suicide. What part of 'fine' did I want to keep and expand on? What part of me wanted to create a phenomenal experience? That bit, just beyond my reach, what was that? What was that extraordinary thing that made me, me? Who could I become?

Oh, this amazing, frustrating, painful, ecstatic, roller-coaster of a journey. I am so incredibly thankful for all of it; the most profound pain and the most blissful joy. I have uncovered my deepest fears, discovered that I had told myself false stories about what I am capable of and who I am, these stories that do not serve my highest good. I have learned there is a voice inside of me that is dying to be heard. And I have decided that it is time to speak.

Suicide is a choice. It was Jeff's choice—one that I will never fully understand. And I have my own choice. I can allow his death to keep me (and our girls) simply surviving for the rest of our lives, or I can use it as an opportunity to celebrate the gift of life. A chance to say, "I choose my life" and a chance to demonstrate to my daughters that choosing to live an intentional, joyful, fulfilling life full of relationships that share unconditional love *is* possible.

I choose to rise. And when I rise, I thrive.

Ashamed
By Shamegan Smith

I've done many different things in my life and have taken ownership of those things. Sometimes some things happen in life where you are one of the involved parties, but the result is no fault of your own. This statement may not make sense to many, but it is very accurate. I was 17 and very naïve, and I met someone, and we became good friends. It eventually evolved into more than just a friendship after three years. I still had my innocence, and I thought he was the one. I thought I was in love. I did not have a mother or a father around to be an example of love.

There was something that I did not know—he was gay. We stayed in a relationship with each other for years, and we were still best friends. I was in love. Seven years later we were both 24 years old. We were on a romantic trip in August 2007 and he told me that he met someone. My heart dropped to my feet, and I did not know what to say or do. I asked who it was, and he was not forthcoming with the truth.

I left the situation alone, but he wanted to remain friends, against my better judgment. I stayed friends with him. He still would not share with me who this mystery person was. I found out he was gay on December 2007, the way I found out was beyond hurtful, and I felt ashamed. I found out by playing a game via text message. A question was forwarded to me. It said, "Tell me something about yourself that no one knows" and I sent the question to him. His response was, "You are going to be mad at me, and I cannot tell you."

So, I began to play the guessing game with him. My first guess was that he had another baby on the way; that answer was wrong. My next guess was something that I didn't expect. I asked him if he was gay. His reply was "yes," and he began to laugh about the situation. How could I not realize that I had slept with a man that was in the closet? It was upsetting that he didn't feel safe enough to tell me the truth. I would accept him no matter what, but the way I found out was hurtful. The fact that he couldn't tell me himself and I had to guess about it was even more harmful.

I became ashamed and scared of my future. My ex-boyfriend was someone I thought I knew. For the next seven years, I walked around with shame as if I did something wrong. It was hard to trust anyone, and relationships were out of the question.

My self-esteem was low, and I couldn't imagine anyone loving me, not even God. Once I realized the truth, I became free. First, I forgave myself and then forgave him for being dishonest. I realized that there was nothing that I did wrong. God showed me a different way of doing things through forgiveness of myself and others. It was indeed about his journey and acceptance of himself and not about me.

Redefining Pain
By Sanya Minocha

I Fell—hard—but I got right back up. And then I fell again.

Does this sound familiar? You fall, and then you get back up.

While this may be the reality for most, my fall was literal. I fell down some stairs, more than once, while surrounded by strangers. I found it easier to brush it off than to feel the pain that was arising at that moment. It was physical pain followed by deep emotional despair. 'Here we go again,' I thought. Once again, life had screwed me over.

This fall, on the 31st of December 2014, would result in me flying higher than ever before. But obviously, I didn't know that at the time. It took almost three years to realize that I was being called to awaken to my magnificence; to see myself as a creator. I didn't know I had been viewing my life through the lens of a victim! But the fall was a calling from my soul. Once I finally made the connection, everything changed. The fall created a burning desire within me to experience myself as a creator. But before I stepped into my new role, I first had to let go of the weight of my past.

With every single throb and ache of my tailbone, I felt my heart aching. With every single tear that I shed, I felt my soul cry. After years of suffering, I realized that my pain was a physical manifestation of the emotional distress I carried with me for over 27 years. And the most surprising part was that it wasn't solely my pain. It was my family's pain. It was the pain of my ancestors. I realized just how much I had been suppressing. After the fall, I began a quest for healing and feeling.

The most remarkable thing about pain is not the actual sensations that arise, but our response to those sensations. We have some very unhelpful default settings in place when we face a tough situation or experience a negative emotion. We immediately want to rid ourselves of that discomfort. We attach immense meaning to our pain, and before we know it, we're feeling even more upset than before. We see our life as a 'failure' only because we're not feeling happy in the moment.

I've come to realize that pain is not the enemy. It's a call to care for and treat ourselves better. It's a call to wake us up to our divinity. It occurs when, at some level, either in the body, mind or spirit, we are not aligned with our true nature. When we resist pain, we think we know better than the intelligence that governs our bodies. All that pain (emotional or physical) asks us to be open to it, without needing to change it.

Now, my definition of the word 'pain' has changed significantly. From being a word that embodies extreme discomfort and negativity to one that is here to transmit a message: "Pay Attention, Integrate Now."

Over the years, I learned that this message wasn't just for my healing. My journey has expanded from a solo mission to a collective purpose. If I can leave you with only one piece of advice about the pain you may be feeling, it would be this: be present with your pain. When sadness comes to visit, hold it. When anger comes to visit, listen to it. And know that one day you'll look back and see that your pain wasn't blocking your path—it is the path.

To My Little Girl
By Christine Do

I have been out in the forest, sitting in a circle shaped from branches and leaves. I have been sitting for hours, thinking about my life. This journey was a quest to find the answers within me, without any distractions, without the usual subtle addictions that take me away from my true self. Alone I have no obligations, no have-to-dos. This was my time to not have to be in service to others and to serve me, unapologetically. So now what? I was all on my own in some eucalyptus forest of rural Australia.

There was space now for me to breathe and to see. Something deep down within me, a desperate longing forced its way to the surface. It finally had a chance to be revealed. I allowed the calcified, hardened shell that protected me to shatter and break apart. My mask split into two and fell to the sides; I was rendered helpless without my 'have to be strong' front. I crumbled. I crawled into a ball. I allowed myself to be hopelessly vulnerable for the first time. A sudden realization hit me. 'Who Am I?' I internally screamed as this encrusted mask cracked away, losing all sense of my familiar identity. I broke down. '*What* have I been all this time?'

In that moment where everything thing fell away, I recalled my childhood. I didn't have any positive role models growing up. Both parents were in prison, and I was taken in by an unwelcoming caregiver. As a child, the environment I knew, and the people around me, was not a happy one. It created deep wounds of feeling unwanted, rejected, abandoned and deeply unlovable. These feelings laid the foundations of my personality, thus driving my fears and motives in life. From my child's mind, I did not want to be like the adults around me, as I saw them as 'bad.' I was the 'Matilda' in a dysfunctional family, and I sought escapism in my books. The only way I knew to define myself and how to be in the world was to not be like the adults in my life: angry, controlling, violent, loud, mean and bossy. These qualities were pushed far into my shadow.

Remember the encyclopedias that were in volumes and were stored alphabetically on the shelf. I recall a scene that changed the course of my life. I ended up in the 'F' edition and found Sigmund Freud. He theorized that our childhood shapes our adulthood and relationships. I suddenly stopped reading, and I looked around at my surroundings. I was only seven years old, and I already knew that my childhood was grim. It didn't make me sad as I had become numb with all the changes and lack of support, my only thought was getting by each day. That was the day I had made a promise to myself. I would never let my environment shape me; I would rise above it. I would not be a product of my childhood.

Twenty years later, I am sitting opposite a therapist. She asks me, "Why are you here?" I reply, "I don't know, my throat is blocked." On a piece of paper, she writes '*childhood*,' and then all the memories of my little girl comes flooding back. I cried so hard and for many days after. I cried for the little girl that could not cry at the time. The wounds have opened again, and once more, my little girl is seen. Through her, she holds the key to my heart. Through her, I thrive.

An Invitation to Simply Be:
Sensory Edition
By Sherry Hess

What happens when we take time to be? As you are reading this message, it isn't possible to be; you are reading, comprehending, and evaluating the shapes of letters on a page. You are learning, not being.

Can you find a place, space and the time to be? Until you experience it, these words will only reside in your mind, and the experience of being will be only a thought. A thought is independent of being. Belief can only affect being when it's believed.

How does being feel? Being is. It's the presence. It's not the thought of presence, or even being in the present. It's a simple existence. It is the miraculous functions of your human body. It is all that we take for granted in our daily life of doing, thinking, learning and deciding. Being is the gift given at birth to experience the world in presence.

Our bodies are our miracle of being. In our world of striving to be significant, heard, accepted or loved on a daily basis, we take for granted the nature of our bodies. You can't command a thought for your lungs to breathe. You can't will your heart to stop nor can you concentrate so hard that you can't feel pain. If a thought creates wonder about blindness, you don't have to fear that it will happen. As I model the importance of my senses in my work, it is critical to recognize that thoughts do not control my senses. Sensing is a part of our being.

Why aren't we paying attention to all of our senses with complete and utter urgency? Sight, sound, touch, and hearing are given great significance to their sensory input. Why not taste? Food and nutrition have become a victim of over-thinking, learning, doing, educating, and re-learning. In the equation of eating, being has been taken out. As a result, we are confused, and our bodies are broken. We don't know what we need because the knowledge is continually changing.

No proven knowledge defines our being. There is little evidence out there about nutrition that hasn't been disputed, over-processed, scientifically dissected and re-routed into a different thought. When we ignore our sense of taste as a tool for the nutrition we need, we are allowing thoughts to dictate our choices.

Unlike the other senses, our sense of taste is in our complete control. You cannot decide what colors you want to see today, what you want the weather to feel like on your skin, or even how your teenager's laundry smells. You can, however, decide what you want to taste today. It's the sense that requires input or action beyond being. But, I challenge you with this thought: Are you allowing your God-given state of being to guide your input, or are you letting the views, education, and rules of engagement to overrule this superpower of taste?

I believe we are missing this giant piece of the puzzle. When it comes to individualized personal health, we need to be, understanding that flavors like salty, sour, sweet, bitter, and umami are all flavors that send messages to our bodies. The critical requirement is flavor from thriving living sources. The flavor can only speak when it comes from life. Only then can it talk to our bodies with in-depth efficiency. Allow the presence of being to power the action of feeding your body.

Living flavor supports joyful being.

Dancing with Imaginary Partners
By Jaklyn Brockman

I used to have a four post white canopy bed when I was a child, and behind closed doors I would dance with the four posts, pretending they were all different dance partners. I felt free. I felt alive. I felt beautiful. But the minute I heard any noise approaching from the hallway, I would turn back into my quiet, obedient Cinderella-like self. I use to say to myself, "I can't wait until someday I can show everyone who I am. All I need is the right partner to free me." Yes, even as a small child, I could recognize my absence of confidence. I didn't know who I truly was, I was waiting around for someone else to show me.

I was born into a Ballroom dancing family. My mother, stepfather, siblings, and an aunt and an uncle were in the business of Ballroom dancing. I felt fortunate to have been given this opportunity even though it meant huge shoes I would have to fill. I was a shy, good-hearted, overly intuitive little girl. I only wanted to make people smile with my light-hearted humor and please everyone by doing and saying the right things.

I continued my life for many years dancing behind closed doors. As I grew into my teens and had my first significant boyfriend, I started to speak up more for myself. As I began to speak up, I noticed for the first time I felt resistance from my parents and felt the lack of confidence they had in me. I started to realize that the person they thought I was, was not the person I thought I was. And so the journey began.

I competed in dance with my stepfather from age 6-18 years old. As I started to turn from a girl into a woman, I found myself blocked with the challenges of being sexy while dancing with my dad! I felt like everyone in the industry looked at me like I was still that cute little 6-year-old girl, the spitting image of my already well-accomplished mother. Not only was I trapped behind those illusive doors choreographing endless routines that no one would ever see, I was stuck in the shade of my mother's shadow.

I went to a small liberal arts college my freshman year and shared a dorm with 35 other girls. If there was any time to find my voice, now was that time! It was catty and corrupt, with small-minded country girls. I loved every minute of it. When I returned home after only one year away, I was a different person. I had a personality. I had opinions of my own, on topics of my own. I had spunk and was sassy and flirty and fun. I had an extra 30 lbs. on me, and I still felt beautiful. The only problem was, I wasn't close with my dad anymore. My world no longer revolved around my family and I had a point of view about everything! I was no longer the "yes ma'am-no ma'am" daughter from when I had left. I had kicked down my door, and I was jumping up and down on it! I was free! And I never looked back. I began running through life like Rapunzel through the forest. Of course, this was just the beginning of a lifetime journey of kicking down doors and reinventing myself over and over again.

To this day I am still Waltzing to my own violin. Sometimes it feels like I have lived ten lifetimes in just the past few decades. I think of who I might be if I was still dancing with imaginary partners like so many people do. Are you waiting for someone to open the door and reveal your soul to the world?

We are all beautiful, and we all have a story to tell. Do not dim your light while others are around. Be proud of who you have become, because you are perfection. Be the light that leads the way when others cannot see. And don't forget to dance! Dance as though everyone is watching.

Finding Lost
By Mariah Ehlert

He wasn't answering the phone.
Could he be lost at sea on his boat?
Ridiculous. Who gets lost at sea these days!

But, the possibility was there. The feeling started in my gut and quickly wrapped around my heart and left me gasping. My father missed my graduation for my master's that past weekend, and the jerk never called or wrote, not even an email. Typical.

A 70-year old man was trying to re-live his glory days in Central America, sailing, gambling, drinking, dating young women. He was living his dream, my father. We weren't close, not like the "daddy" I'd wanted him to be: adoring, loving, and doting.

How the hell do you sleep when your parent is missing without a trace? He was lost. My inner child felt abandoned, and I spiraled. How can I heal this internal agony? Where and how did he die? How can I find his body in another country? How do I cut a chunk of couch off for a blood sample? Where could I get a DNA sample to test? I couldn't give any DNA because I was adopted. Does anyone on this flight realize my purse contains a piece of a couch soaked in blood? Will he miraculously appear and hate me for not finding him? For taking control of all his accounts and going through his files?

Stuck.

It was difficult managing my stress and trauma. My life was going horribly. My health was out the door, systemic inflammation, always sick, and sleep-prohibitive nightmares. Hermit-scale isolation was creeping in. Going out wasn't fun. Either I faced well-meaning, but sad-faced pity, or questions, so many questions. Why even bother to venture out? And do I deserve to have a life or have fun when he's still missing? What's the statute on 'missing parent: having fun again'? Months? Years?

The story became public and, gratefully, help found me. Incredible healers gently helped me stand up again. I learned how and why my body and my brain were crawling into a cave. My heart lifted. I learned how to meditate with a directed focus to stop re-traumatizing myself every day; how to stop the nightmares.

It was marathon-like training; only the finish line was my health, my life, my joy. I permitted myself to let go. I forgave him and myself. I imagined him coming to me, in peace and love with pride and telling me how much he loved me, and that he was sorry.

Through my struggle, I began to see my strength. This struggle was the blessing that helped me bloom, heal, and grow. I came into my power. I sold my house, then bought and renovated an old church. Got laid off from my six-figure job, and dove into entrepreneurship; something fear would have prevented previously.

This new uncertain life brought new levels of anxiety. However, I refused to go backward. I would not suffer. It was only perceived stress, created in my mind. Knowing this, I worked with brain science and my belief in a brilliant future.

Struggle, I taught myself, doesn't have to mean suffering. Soaring, I was safe, safe to embrace a happier life, which allowed my savvy limbic brain relief from a 24/7 schedule. My creative, eager, beautiful pre-frontal cortex thrived.

Life opened up like a beautiful giant butterfly. Uncertainty transformed from fear into possibilities and potential. Although I never found him, I did find myself. Thank you, Pops. I love you.

The Final Gift
By Marion Andrews

Many years ago, my brother-in-law, Jack, lost consciousness while driving on a quiet highway; drove off the road, through a shallow ditch, across a farmer's field, and into the open door of a barn. The diagnosis was a malignant brain tumor—inoperable. He endured radiation treatments, hoping to slow down cancer. After this, the doctors gave him the news that there was nothing more to do.

One day I got the call saying it was time for me to come. It relieved my sister when I arrived, and within hours Jack took a turn for the worse. We called an ambulance to take him to the hospital. "Comfort Care" is the term now used for this end-of-life care. The hospital was more than accommodating. His room was near the doors that led to an area set up for families to rest and have privacy. It had a small kitchen area, a bathroom with shower, a bedroom and an area with comfy sofas and lounge chairs. My sister, her children, I, and other family members spent most of the next ten days right here. Food arrived daily: beautiful meals, snacks, and goodies. A loving daughter-in-law and extended family cared for all of us exceptionally well.

As the days ticked by, Jack's body began the dying process. He would stop breathing for a short period (apnea). This symptom is a common occurrence in the steps leading to that final breath. The body seems to need these practice sessions to shut down. Jack's 96-year-old mother was coming to visit him one afternoon. Although he was in and out of consciousness, I gave him some strict instructions— do not stop breathing while your mother is in the room. It would disturb her to witness this behavior! His daughter and I stood near his bedside while his mother held his hand and spoke softly to him. After some time had passed, we suggested that my sister and other relatives take Grandma to the family comfort area for some tea and cookies. They no sooner left the room when he stopped breathing for what seemed like a long, long time. It was as though he said, "Okay, she is out of here. Now, I can catch up with this non-breathing practice." My niece and I held his hands and thanked him over and over for his exemplary conduct with his mother.

A few days later, I was preparing to fly home. That final morning, my sister and I were there with him. My sister was on the phone with one of her sons. I was alone, holding his hand and quietly told him that I was leaving in a few hours. I said that if he wanted me to be there for his passing, he needed to go soon. The most glorious thing happened shortly after. A look of beautiful peace and joy came over his face. He was looking into the distance with a big smile lighting up his face. He held my hand. I felt and witnessed his life force leave his body. It was a profound and sacred experience! To this day, I get goosebumps all over and feel so humbled by this.

My privilege and blessing were that I could be there to be present for my brother-in-law, my sister, my nieces and nephews at this wonder-filled time to witness a loving and loved spirit of life exit this frail body of bones to go back to the world of love and light.

Mirror, Mirror On The Wall
By Kyra Schaefer

There was a time in my life when I was severely depressed. Everywhere I looked I saw nothing but sadness and pain. I heard people talking about how bad things were. I listened to the news showing me the world falling apart. There was evidence everywhere that continued to reinforce my bad feelings. Any time I looked in the mirror I saw nothing of importance or significance. I was tired of feeling badly, so I decided to go against my programming. Every day I woke up and looked in the mirror and said, "I am beautiful." What happened next was surprising.

Day 1: Looking in the Mirror

Kyra: I am beautiful.

Kyra's mind: That's a lie, you're disgusting and ridiculous. This is a stupid exercise.

Kyra: I guess you're right, I'm not beautiful.

Day 2: Looking in the Mirror

Kyra: I am beautiful.

Kyra's mind: You've got to be kidding me; this crap again? I'll never believe that, just look at yourself. Stupid.

Kyra: Uh, I'm not sure about this exercise.

Day 3: Looking in the Mirror

Kyra: I am beautiful.

Kyra's mind: Seriously? Didn't you hear me? You suck.

Kyra: You know what, shut the hell up. I'm tired of you telling me who I am.

Kyra's mind: Well, what good is this doing? You still aren't good enough.

Kyra: I don't care what you think. Back off.

Day 4: Looking in the Mirror

Kyra: I am beautiful.

Kyra's mind: Ugh...

Kyra: Zip it!

Day 5: Looking in the Mirror

Kyra: I am beautiful.

Kyra's mind: Fine. You're okay, I guess.

Kyra: Damn right!

Day 6: Looking in the Mirror

Kyra: I am beautiful.

Kyra's mind: Hmm, that feels pretty good.

Kyra: That's right! I am beautiful. Say it, bitch. Beautiful!

Kyra's mind: Okay, okay. You're beautiful.

Kyra: Say it like you mean it.

Kyra's mind: You are beautiful! Happy now?

Kyra: Almost.

Day 7: Looking in the Mirror

Kyra: I am beautiful! (Dancing and twirling around)

Kyra's mind: …

Kyra: Ahhhh, peace.

I think the process took more than seven days, but it is possible to consciously recondition the subconscious mind by going against that inner programming that consistently puts you down.

Another way to go against your programming can be very simple. You could take a different route to work. You could take a trip somewhere you've never been. If you usually say, "No" to going out with friends, say, "Yes" instead. If you are a people-pleaser like me, start saying "No" to people who take from you.

You benefit from going backwards to going forwards. You benefit from going completely opposite to your normal patterns.

I have a client who always puts everyone else first, even when it hurts her career or her health. She has put the needs of her boss, her husband and her children first. You may think to yourself, "How selfless, how amazing she must feel good to be such a giver." Well, there's a difference between being full of love and happily giving of yourself and being asked to do too much and saying yes when you need to say no.

She has been in the hospital and, admittedly, felt it was a nice break where others finally put her needs first. She felt taken care of. This is the most common thing I've seen in women who consistently sacrifice their happiness for others.

They make themselves ill so that they can get away from it all.

Can you imagine always doing something you hate just to make sure everyone else was happy? It's like eating poop because everyone else wants and expects you to do it and like it!

This truth is counterintuitive. Doing more for others and caring less for you actually contributes to those people you serve feeling less loved, not more.

My client decided to fight her programming. She made a choice that immediately put her into a state of anxiety. This is normal. Anyone who goes against what they've always done may feel uncomfortable at first, but that doesn't mean something good isn't happening. It profoundly changes your brain. It changes your environment and others' responses to you.

At first, the people around you will feel shaky with the newfound empowerment you place upon them to care for themselves. Then, people will notice they are making their own breakfasts, washing their own clothes, finishing their own projects, watching their own children, and overall, being inconvenienced by not doing what they've always done—having you take care of their every need. You may encounter some resistance from them; stay strong.

They will learn a very important lesson—one that everyone needs to learn. You rob them of self-reliance by sacrificing yourself.

When I was three years old, my father was killed. He made choices that consistently put him in physical danger.

That's all that needs to be said, because it isn't as important to me as my mother's reaction to his death and what it meant to my self-reliance.

My mother admitted to me recently the reason she was strict and made me do so much as a child was because she was afraid that if something happened to her, I would have no one and would be left alone to fend for myself. This was a tremendous gift she gave me. I can't imagine I would lead the blessed life I do without the lessons she taught me.

I knew how to cook, do dishes, fold clothes, dust, start a fire (with gasoline, but that's a different story), vacuum, manage money (if something looks the same and costs less, go for the less expensive), change diapers, and feed babies (how much and how often). I knew how to paint walls, and deep clean carpets. I learned how to make money in a variety of ways that cost nothing but time and elbow-grease. I knew about death, and how pets come in and out of our lives like people do; so love them as much as possible while they are here.

I learned that people aren't always trustworthy, but as long as you know how to defend yourself, people won't take advantage of you. It may sound bad, but it helped me to be in alignment with myself and remember that as much as I love people, there are still folks that are confused about their self-worth and will rob, cheat and steal to get what they want.

I learned all of this and consistently practiced it by the time I was eight years old. I was an expert, as long as I didn't have to reach things too far above my head. Even then, I would climb on the counter top to get whatever I wanted.

It wasn't always fun, because it took work. I only did it because I wanted to please my mom. Believe me, I gave my mom the normal grunts and groans from any child, but she didn't care. She created some significant consequences if my simple desire for her love wasn't enough.

No matter how others grunt and groan at you for encouraging them to be responsible, requiring them to treat you with respect and simply loving yourself more in the process, your friends and family will feel more loved as a result. There is no love in a "sacrifice-win" situation. Only a "win-win" will feel loving to everyone involved.

Life After Suicide
By Kelsey Quattlebaum

I have struggled with depression for as long as I can remember. I started having thoughts of suicide by age 12. The most challenging thing about these thoughts is once they've started, they never seem to stop. I would go about life and no matter how amazing things got, the moment the rug was ripped out from under me I was back in that place. I experienced that dark, lonely place where I didn't want to live anymore. After 12 years of battling this demon, I chose to swallow every pill I could find. Although the story of how I got to this place is essential, it's no longer the story I need to tell.

Four days after the incident I was finally able to dress, and although shaking, I stood up and stepped outside for the first time. I sat on the stoop and began formulating a plan. 'One step at a time,' I said to myself. Three days later, I was pulling my 1973 Security Traveler (camper) to our new home. It was time to lay a new foundation, both physically and emotionally. I was starting at ground zero. It felt as though the year and a half of soul searching and personal development I had done before the 11-month relationship was completely wiped. Every week, my Life Coach and Shaman reminded me that wasn't true. In the eye of the storm, at the very center of this hurricane, was a truth—I still didn't love myself.

I wove a necklace, binding into it the promise to deeply, truly, genuinely love myself. As I began the work, layer after layer has revealed to me what that means. Old demons resurfaced. I experienced pain from my childhood as if I was reliving it. Layer after layer, I was asked the question, "Can you love yourself here?" And layer after layer, I have. While sorting through one of these layers, I found myself in a deep, trance-like meditation. After spending hours in this state, a voice whispered into my right ear, "South America." Memories flashed, moments in my history when South America seemed to be calling. I didn't grasp to this idea with giddy excitement—quite the opposite. For once in my life, I wasn't running from anything. There were no thoughts of travel on my horizon. I was longing to grow roots and have a family, a place to belong. I spent two weeks wrestling with this calling, and despite my frustration, I decided I wasn't going to ignore the messages. I understood and accepted that I would be leaving for Chile in three and a half months.

The moment I said yes every single detail fell into place as if a travel agent had planned the entire process for me. I have a one-way ticket to Santiago, Chile. I'll be staying and working at a retreat center for a minimum of six weeks. The Universe has assisted me in manifesting $6,000 in two months. Everything I own fits inside my home on wheels. She is safely stored, waiting for my unknown return.

Although I have a slight idea of what this journey will bring, I have released all expectations. I've released the desire to plan or control what is unfolding. I wake up every morning happy to be alive, wanting to be alive. I have free fallen into the divine love of the Universe knowing without a shadow of a doubt that guidance will be available to me every step of the way. 'One step at a time.'

Answer The Door
By Joi Hayes

"Mom, that was the doorbell, Mom are you getting the door?" No, I thought because no good news has come from opening the door lately. With the divorce pending and nosy neighbors, everyone wanting something from me that I can't seem to give. No, I am not getting the door, maybe they will go away.

An envelope is dropped into my lap by a not so happy teenager. What now? It is December, and I have not put up decorations or sent Christmas cards. Divorce takes so much from people; it steals the joy that the holidays used to bring.

I absentmindedly opened the envelope and pulled the cheery card out, and five crisp 100 dollar bills fell into my lap. The sender knew everything that was going on, and I burst into tears. 'I can't take this, how could they do this, I am so embarrassed they know we don't have much this year,' I thought to myself.

I recall how my mother always taught us to give. She made bread weekly and gave the extra loaves away. One Christmas she came home and told us that she just spoke to a woman with five children who were buying soup for Christmas dinner; no presents for her children. She gathered us up and asked if we would be willing to give up our supper, presents, and stockings for this family. How could we say no? We didn't have much ourselves at that time in our lives. Though we felt blessed because we had everything we needed. We put everything in a box and put it on the doorstep, rang the doorbell and hid. We saw the wonder and joy on the faces of that family. The next morning we had the sweetest breakfast of bread and milk and peaches, my Mom had canned. Love filled our hearts, and we were grateful we could give to someone else.

I remember teaching my daughters the same thing. When they were 5 and 6, they painted rocks, which they took from the neighbors' yard, then set up a stand to sell them. The neighbors bought back the stones, which they kept in their window sill to this day. My daughters bought tennis shoes for a woman in the projects who only wore slippers. I then remembered my daughter asking if she could give her bike to someone at work; it was his only form of transportation; she was 17 at the time. Or how about the Christmas jars we put change in all year, added $100.00 and gave to someone who needed it.

Now it was me in need, but I didn't want 'charity.' My daughter looked me in the eyes and said, "Mom, you always give, you taught us to give. It is okay to say thank you and be grateful. I know when you are back on your feet you will start giving again." These were the words of an angel whom I raised. I was so proud of her, I hugged her and felt my mom's arms around us both.

I went to my room, got on my knees and thanked my Heavenly Father for angels who loved me enough to share what they had. Gratitude and Love filled my heart.

Rocking Out With My Teeth Out
By Carlyn Shaw

October 2013: I stood in the bathroom staring at myself in the mirror. How did I let this happen?

My unrecognizable face was swollen, scabbed, bruised and broken. But, for the first time in four months, my body, my spirit, and my soul felt everything.

The backstory:

I wanted friendship; he seemed smitten at first sight. I have "Love Life" tattooed on the back of my neck. He adorned the label "widower." While our chemistry was off the charts, our spiritual connection was nonexistent. He said "I love you." I nodded in agreement.

Terrified of my truth, I remained silent. Rather than follow my heart, I fought my intuition. I traded my life for his.

One evening we went to a concert. I didn't want to go. Instead, I went, which resulted in the breaking of my right foot and spirit. While at the hospital, the nurse told me I was pregnant while being prepped for foot surgery. I left the hospital more broken than I arrived. My gut knew the risk of our ravenous sex life. My intuition knew what to do. Instead, I searched outside myself and dragged us through the mud. I finally got an abortion on my fourth attempt.

Three weeks and six days later:

I didn't want to go to the football game. I again didn't follow my intuition and catapulted off of my bike. I face-planted on the pavement, shattered my front teeth on impact and forcefully flipped on my back. My eyes locked with the one cloud in a bright blue sky. I surrendered.

Painfully sipping my breath, I gasped at my reflection. Like a dormant volcano, my emotions erupted from the pit of my stomach. Lips destroyed and glued together with bloody scabs and open sores. I finally permitted myself to cry, to wail, to sob. Accepting my new reality, I began to mourn for myself.

Like tributaries of grief, my tears found their way into the small crevices of my puffy cheeks. The anger. The sadness. The regret. The longing. The mercy. The release.

When I rise, I thrive:

Three years prior, I bought my favorite white t-shirt. In black typewriter font stretched across the chest reads, "Whoever Smiles First Wins." I never imagined wearing it without teeth.

Though it would take several weeks before I smiled comfortably without wincing in pain, smile, I did! I called it, "Rocking Out With My Teeth Out." You see, everyone reached out to check on me. Rather than hide in shame, I posted photos on social media. Having hidden for so long, this was my time to step out in truth, to shift my story and be seen. Also, going through hell and back, I took life a little less seriously. Life could break me, rob me, smack me upside the face, but it could never steal my spirit, my smile.

Perspective is everything. It turns out love and laughter genuinely are the best medicine.

Weeks later, I choose my Halloween costume, "All I want for Christmas is my two front teeth." For Christmas, I waited in line with the kiddos to sit on Santa's lap. I turned my frown upside down and flashed my crooked grin for all the world to see.

To share my self-love and the silver linings of my tooth loss, I published a blog, "Top 5 Lessons Learned From Losing My Two Front Teeth." I read the book, "The Gift of Imperfection" by Brené Brown. At the time of my accident, I quoted what she wrote on social media. She tweeted about my experience to her audience with the word "Brave." To this day, men and women seek me for comfort in their own teeth loss journey.

Reigniting the Fire
By Nick Browning

C hallenges don't stop in this life, in fact, they come faster the older that you get. What was once a challenge in childhood has now become a luxury in adulthood. There are so many aspects of life that can get more complicated; it's only natural that our problems follow us down that path as well. I think back to many difficulties with friends, family, school, and work, however, there is one in my adult life that stands above them all—a partner who shattered my trust. If we are to have a semblance of meaningful relationships, including the relationship with ourselves, we must seize the opportunity of broken trust. Yes, I said opportunity, because that's honestly what a situation like this is, despite not wanting to believe that for so long.

The thing is that I loved her so much that it blinded my innate trust and intuition. It started at the end of summer when the air was still warm and reassuring, not biting at your face as it does in winter. It was right for the time. We were inseparable. At one point, her parents even told me that this was the happiest that they had ever seen her. I was finishing up graduate school. We talked for many late nights after I completed my work. I learned she was at least satisfied with her job at a local hospital, but not necessarily happy in life. Her self-loathing and self-hatred began to creep in. I didn't know how to talk to her anymore. I just wanted her to see herself as I did. As months went on and the holiday season moved in, I started to notice little things that began to put a crack in the foundation of trust that we had laid months before. Always being tired to the point where she didn't even want to get dinner after work, go to the park, or take a walk, she had physical symptoms that one cannot ignore. I just figured it was the job and the stress. The lies began, both big and small.

She overdosed on the morning of December 17th, the night we were supposed to leave on a trip together. I had no idea. I lost two best friends to overdoses, but she didn't die. As she lay in the hospital bed paralyzed, I knew I was witnessing an overdose. I talked with friends and family who told me to leave, to get as far as I could from her and this situation due to the level of broken trust. She was the first person in my life to overdose and come back from it, so I stayed. Looking back on it, I should have left; I should have said my piece and went a different way and confronted the challenge of building my trust again immediately. Instead, I stayed to the point where my trust was eventually shattered like a champagne flute violently hitting concrete.

The challenge eventually evolved into trusting my mind and others again after being brutally broken, picking the pieces of myself up and slowly fitting them back together. It took time, crying, mental effort, and a deep dive into myself. It took reassuring phone calls with family and friends that everything would be okay, eventually. My relationships with friends and family were the catalyst in overcoming this challenge. However, I held the gas and matches to tear down and rebuild my trust in others simultaneously.

Thank You
By Serissa Asta

My story seems to be the same over and over again.

And I think all of our stories are only stories.

We are all connected; I like to believe.

I see you, and you see me. Yes, please.

I'll start with my heart.

I know it could stop at any time, but it continues to
beat and sometimes I wonder why?

I often question, what defines me?

What am I without my pain?

Who am I without my stories?

I felt so punished I tried to kill myself once.

I was tired of aching.

I didn't know what to do with myself,

how to love me,

and that there was more than what I've been shown.

Who is underneath it all?

Who am I beyond what you want me to be?

Without you.

The hoops.

I carried the weight from those who have owned me.

I was a slave.

I am scattered like a seed now.

I have bloomed.

You don't own me, and you can't find me.

I see my beauty

Yea

Mmmmm

I love to feel the Sun.

I love to be watered.

I love to grow.

I wouldn't be here without you.

Thank you.

One Part Of The Journey
By Tammy Coin

As a woman who has overcome multiple traumas, abuses and challenges since birth, I thought I understood faith. I didn't.

In October 2016, I was at a critical point. I was physically and emotionally ill and was breaking down. I needed someone to take the reins for a little while so that I could recover. I needed my husband more than I had ever needed anyone. Instead of taking control for us, he stopped believing in me, and he left. I was alone.

This act created a ripple effect inside my body. For the first time in my life, there were no children, no men, no family or pets to distract me. It was just me. I was alone.

After everything I had been through, I was spiraling, and I could not make it stop. Every single fear, pain, trauma, abuse that I had endured and stuffed in my body for 51 years came at me like a freight train. For someone with a Complex Post Traumatic Stress Disorder diagnosis and severe abandonment issues, this isn't the best combination.

For two months, I laid in that empty house and moaned like a wounded animal. I stood in the mirror and screamed at myself. I was fractured. I was fragmented. These pieces that I had held so delicately together for an entire lifetime were crumbling.

Meanwhile, I would make it out into the world or the online space from time to time, putting on the best face I could, explaining my financial situation here and there, but never fully able to disclose what was happening to me. I still held space for others.

Then, I would return to that empty house, curl in a fetal position and listen to lullabies in an attempt to soothe all these wounded children coming out of my body. The core of my self-abandonment became exposed, and I could no longer hide it from myself. The self-loathing came pouring out of me like lava from a volcano—every word burning me from the inside out.

The fear of survival was real. I was incapable during that period of being employed or getting anyone that I shared with to fully understand the Hell I was living. I was alone. By Western standards, I could have gotten diagnosed and placed in the hospital. I fought suicidal thought daily for almost two years. I became my Healer.

I connected with myself, my Higher Self, Spirit, Great Spirit and God (there's a lot of us when we get together!). I was living on faith and miracles.

Every skill I had ever acquired in my life came to the surface to help me. I began to love and heal all those wounded children who lived inside me. I listened and spoke to God daily.

On September 2, 2018, I was Divinely guided to begin a road trip. The road trip ended on November 28, 2018. I had stayed in 14 homes and drove a total of 6,066 miles. During the faith-based road trip, it was imperative to remain fully present in every moment. Soulfully relying on myself and

Spirit. Never knowing if I would have shelter, food, or income.

The connection I made with me over these past two years was profound. I have learned the value of self-love. I have learned my worth. I have learned to enjoy the time spent alone. I have learned to believe in myself so much that it no longer matters if anyone else believes in me. Being divinely guided is important, and I listen. I have faith. I take inspired action, and I leap.

We Came to Buy a Cow, They Wanted a School
By Katie Hilborn

Traveling through the Himalayan foothills at night by bus might not be the safest method of travel. The road ahead is winding; it can be assumed there is a 500-foot drop on one side. The only thing I can see are the headlights from an oncoming bus as it swerves back into its lane to avoid a near-miss collision.

Though dangerous, night travel was inevitable as our twenty-hour journey brought us from the Himalayan foothills to the jungle lowlands near the Indian border. As we stepped off the bus, the humidity began to stir-fry our brains as a single sweat bead rolled off our foreheads. It was like an oven—hot and miserable, one-hundred degrees with moisture, and miles from anything remotely considered civilization.

The villagers of Udaipur welcomed us with open arms. Wood huts on stilts, above water-filled rice fields, added to my intrigue. They were happy to see us, as my Nepalese friend brought me to see how I could help. After purchasing cows to give families a form of sustainability months prior, I thought this was a perfect way to spend the remaining fund.

So you will understand my surprise when all they wanted was a primary school.

"Um, Dipak, why exactly do these people think I am here?" I asked inquisitively. "Do they think I am coming to build a school?'

"Oh yes, yes Katie, see how you can help. No worries," he replied casually.

But the fact remained that they indeed wanted a school. They had enough cows to last them a lifetime. The $500 that I brought with me for the purchase of a cow was erroneous. Had I traveled all this way for nothing?

I was disappointed but ate my curry dinner that was so eloquently prepared, and the following morning I woke with a bout of E.coli.

Nothing is more enjoyable in life than being plagued with a stomach bug in 100-degree heat with no toilets or running water, and pooping your pants.

I was miserable and nauseous; I couldn't even pull myself up from the straw bed. But still, the villagers insisted that I make the 40-minute journey to the school site the following day on foot for a preliminary visit.

The walk was long and arduous. Fainting under the jungle sun five minutes prior was my last straw. Going in-and-out of coherency, I questioned my decision of ever leaving the city. As I sat in the grass, a large crowd of one-hundred people were waiting for me.

"Oh my God! Quick, full power," I exclaimed as a Nepalese lady fanned my face, putting my hair into a ponytail.

I was walking into a ceremony, and I couldn't even stand on my own! I splashed some water on my face to shake it off and on we went with a person holding me up by each arm. They adorned us with flower necklaces, and each child presented a gift. I felt like I was hallucinating from a combination of the heat, the illness, and the fact that I was in the strangest place and participating in a ceremony so foreign.

I tried to stay collected as long as possible but eventually ran off the stage to vomit into the bush. I felt children holding my hair and an elderly woman rubbing my back. A few days later of rest allowed me to start eating again and collect my thoughts.

The village needed a primary school. The elders knew it was the only way for their generations to escape the endless cycle of hard, manual labor. They work the rice plantations from the time they can walk until the day they die.

I was in no position financially or resourcefully to build a school. I am just one woman. How could they expect some backpacker like me to create a school for an entire village?

It was inconceivable, but just as serendipitous moments often occur, there was a secret donor amongst our group. My French travel companion unclipped his Buddhist necklace from around his neck and placed it on mine.

"It means invincible," he said. "Whoever wears it is just that. Take my 1,000 Euros and construct a foundation. Then come back and finish it."

Are You Little Happy Or Big Happy?
By Marchelle Bentley

D on't tell your children anything—ask questions. Don't tell your children to be the best. Tell them to be the best just for today. Our children will already face enough challenges in life, so adding extra pressure will do nothing for their confidence. One thing that my child went through when she was young was the death of a classmate and friend.

When Ashley was 6 years old, all the children in her class were scheduled to go on a field trip. Ashley was very excited, as were all the children. She went to school as she normally did, happy and interested in learning something new. She did not know the heartbreak that awaited her arrival.

The teacher announced she was preparing for the field trip but had some sad news. All the children listened intently. El Jermain, a classmate, had perished in a house fire along with his brother. This news saddened all of the children, but Ashley was inconsolable. No matter how badly she wanted to stop crying, she simply couldn't. Her teacher tried to make her stop crying by saying, "We are all going to have fun today, and you will be fine." But Ashley shook her head, and continued to cry.

As Ashley was travelling home on the bus, her teacher called me about El Jermain. The teacher told me that Ashley had been "disruptive" all day on the field trip.

"Are you calling me so that I might punish her?" I asked.

"You need to have a talk with her," she said in an interfering tone.

"Are you trying to tell me how to raise my child?" I asked, but before I let her answer, I hung up without a word.

Ashley's uncle Hank worked at the fire department close to where El Jermain had lived, and where the subsequent fire had taken his life. I called uncle Hank to ask him if he knew anything about what happened. Interestingly enough, uncle Hank had been on that call and he carried out a small boy who had died that night. I told him that the boy was Ashley's classmate, El Jermain, whom she had lunch with every day and loved very much.

As a parent, you have to pull from the deepest parts of your soul to help you explain to children that bad things happen, even to other children. Finding ways to do that can be the most challenging and heart-wrenching pursuit.

Although Ashley knew about the concept of death (because her father died when she was 3), it didn't make it any easier to help her understand death when it comes to a child and a close friend. This is how she and I came to terms with this tragedy.

I always read to Ashley, and when I did I tried to help her see other things, not just the lessons in the book. To help her understand death, I told her that everyone has a book of life. Some books may be long with many pages, some are medium sized and some only have one page. Every book is important, even if it's short. Helping her to have seen that life is impermanent (before this tragedy) was valuable. She knew nothing was wrong with death; it was a part of life and it is okay to cry, especially if the book was very short.

When Ashley got off the bus, she and I sat down on the front steps. I looked at my daughter still catching her breath from sadness, her eyes still full of tears, and I said, "You and me, we've got this one, Ashley." That is when I told her that I had called her uncle Hank, the firefighter.

"I talked to your teacher and she told me about El Jermain," I said to my little girl, who was so full of sadness. "When did you feel the saddest today?" I asked her.

"He missed his snack time, and his lunch time, and one snack on the bus ride home," she said with big tears falling on her cheeks.

"I'm going to tell you something, and when I'm done, I want you to tell me if you feel 'little happy' or 'big happy.'

"Okay Momma," she said.

"Do you know uncle Hank went to that fire and put that fire out? Oh, yes he did!" I said and she smiled. "You know what else he did?" I said.

"What?" she replied.

"He carried El Jermain out of that fire."

"He did?" Ashley's eyes widened.

"Oh, yes he did!" I said.

There was a pause and Ashley smiled.

"Why are you smiling?" I asked, uncertain. Then she said something I will never forget.

"Momma, I'm smiling because uncle Hank took El Jermain to heaven."

I had to pause for a moment at the profound innocence of this child. She loved her uncle Hank. She loved El Jermain. In her mind, knowing that her uncle Hank was there meant even though El Jermain was dead, he wasn't alone.

"Now Ashley, answer me something. After learning uncle Hank was there for El Jermain, are you little happy or big happy?"

A smile grew across my child's face. "Big happy," she said.

"That's very brave of you. Do you want to go to McDonalds?"

Ashley nodded.

"Get in the car, let's go," I said.

The next day when she got off the bus, I asked her, "Did you feel little happy or big happy today?"

She responded, "Big happy. I didn't cry at all, but I was sad at lunch time."

My daughter grew up and is now 40 years old. She still remembers El Jermain. To this day, she appreciates that I ask her questions instead of telling her how to think or how to feel. Neither a child nor an adult can feel good when you tell them they will be "fine." Everyone has their own process. They have to explore in order to understand who they are, and they determine when they will be ready to be "fine."

All anyone can do is be their best today. Ashley did her best with the loss. I did my best to help her navigate it, and together we were able to find our "Big Happy."

The Plan
By Todd Schaefer

There's a way of things, a plan.

A way that few choose to understand.

A noble deed that's been unsought,

Can't be seen by those distraught.

The fire that breathes into your soul.

The mindless chatter of days untold.

A righteous way to see the light.

The choice to be made is always one's right.

What can be said of stories untold?

Can you be brave and courageous? Can you be bold?

Stream your thoughts, silence your mind.

Cheers to the days you decide to be kind.

Why is this, the earth of deceit?

Perspective, you see, is how you compete.

Align yours with His; raise your thoughts high.

Be courageous, be bold, never cast aside.

In your heart you'll know that which you must.

Try very hard, and don't live unjust.

Can you see, what life is about?

No frets if you don't, don't scream and pout.

The mind of the mediocre let's his fears decide.

What he'll do next, in passivity or stride.

The mind of man is hard to grasp.

Transform your best efforts, put them in clasp.

No frets, no fears, no underworld place,

Can reveal the high road, the All-Knowing grace.

Live a life of love, a life of goodwill.

God's word is speaking to you, as you are still.

Wonder about being lost? About the life you can't find?

Calm yourself—silence your mind.

God speaks in peace, and not in confusion.

Accepting negativity is exactly the illusion.

Keep it out of your way, aside. Let it stray.

Optimism is the high road, at least I know this today.

What will the answers be? Tomorrow, or the next?

The thoughts you think now, aren't they complex?

Something's afoot! This just can't be!

My thoughts are my reality! What should they be?

Thoughts that propel you forward, not keep you back,

Are the thoughts you should keep especially intact.

You are where you are. Accept this without question.

Claiming who you want to be, is a start and good suggestion.

So for those seeking to learn, and to understand.

Be courageous, be bold, there surely is a plan.

45 Personal Development Questions to Ponder

1. What do you want to accomplish in this life?

2. Have you ever dreamed of having something from your dreams come true?

3. What is the best possible outcome of a current challenge you are facing?

4. If you could make a wish and it come true what would you wish?

5. When looking at a situation do you see possible positive outcomes? What are they?

6. What would you say is the best experience you have ever had?

7. What is your dream job?

8. Who were the villains in your childhood?

9. Who are the villains in your adulthood?

10. What role did your parents play in your life as a child?

11. What role do your parents play in your life now?

12. How often do you do something loving for yourself?

13. When was the last time you treated yourself to something luxurious?

14. When was the last time you offered love to someone who was being unkind?

15. What is the best relationship you have ever had?

16. How often do you reach out to your old friends?

17. When was the last time you told someone you loved them?

18. Who were the heroes of your childhood?

19. Who are your heroes of adulthood?

20. What inspires you?

21. Who inspires you?

22. If it were a perfect world, how would your life be different?

23. If money were no object and you knew you couldn't fail, what would you do differently?

24. If you were to make a wish for someone you care about, what would you wish for them?

25. What could you talk about all day long and not get tired?

26. What could you write about all day long and not get tired?

27. What would you do that seems like work for others but is really fun for you?

28. When you wake up, what is the first thing you do?

29. If you had unlimited resources what would you build?

30. What would the title of your life story be?

31. Write a six word story about your life.

32. Name everything you love.

33. What is your special gift or talent?

34. What is your favorite animal?

35. Do you like to advocate for people, places, or things? What are they?

36. Do you like to dance alone or with a partner?

37. Have you ever sung in public?

38. Would you have a career that caused you to be in the public?

39. What is the most embarrassing thing you have ever experienced?

40. Does being embarrassed matter to you?

41. Would you consider yourself humble?

42. How often do you visit family? Would you like it to be more?

43. What is your deepest regret?

44. If you have a regret, what would you like to do differently?

45. If someone wronged you in the past, can you forgive them now?

Blank Journal Pages

_____

_____

_____

_____

_____

_____

_____

_____

_____

_____

_____

_____

_____

_____

_____

_____

_____

Author Bios

Alicia Sweezer

Alicia Sweezer, Bachelor of Science, is a Nationally Certified Practitioner of Access Consciousness® Bars, Energetic Healings, Clearings, Animal Communication, Intuitive Readings and Mediumship. As a child, she knew she was different than those around her, but she had yet to learn how. Over her lifetime, she learned to interpret and use all the information being presented to her through a variety of forms. She loves connecting with nature and with like-minded people. Using her brilliant intuitive and healing talents, she allows her clients to connect with the Truth of who they really are, bringing their unique gifts and light to the world. Alicia is available for private sessions and group events. To learn more about Alicia and to obtain her services, visit www.whoknewhealing.com or contact her at: alicias@whoknewhealing.com

Andrea Sommer

Andrea Sommer is a single mother to three amazing young ladies. She has shared her story with you in the hopes it helps others to realize it is easier to overcome adversity when we recognize our strengths. Her experience and knowledge is diverse with 18 years combined experience working in the nonprofit sector with women, palliative clients, seniors, and adults with disabilities. She is a writer, blogger who is passionate about healthy living and has received training in Reflexology, Touch for Health, Yoga, and is a Reiki Master. She invites you to connect with her at: andrea_sommer@yahoo.com

Ann Agueli

Ann Agueli is an award-winning/best-selling inspirational author, writer, and coach. Her heartfelt passion and enlightening experiences as a believer in creation and its creator lead her mission. She's called to share divine inspiration and transformational insights through her writing/coaching. You can find Ann's inspirational writings, transformational books, services or contact her for life coaching on her website:
www.theinspiredlivingnetwork.com
https://www.theinspiredlivingnetwork.com/best-sellingawardwinningauthor Ann's Other Books on Amazon: When God Nods: Inspirational Tales of Divine Serendipity Transformational Journaling for Mind, Body, Spirit Joy-Full Journaling for the Caregiver's Spirit: A Transformational Workbook

Anna Pitchouguina's

Anna Pitchouguina's passion for justice and creative expression led her through attaining a Bachelor of Laws, Bachelor of Arts (History major and Philosophy minor) and a Bachelor of Arts Honours, having written an undergraduate thesis on Madame Blavatsky in the field of mysticism. Additionally, Anna competes in Latin, Ballroom and New Vogue styles of dancing. 2018 saw Anna and her dance partner become World Champions in B-Grade Women's Latin Same-Sex Dancesport:
crossingfaith.wordpress.com

Barbara Womack

Barbara Womack and her husband of nearly 35 years have lived in Virginia's beautiful Shenandoah Valley, where they raise sheep, chickens and all sorts of vegetables. They've been vendors at the Staunton Farmers' Market for over 20 years. Barbara is currently working on a memoir about their life journey. You can find more of her writings at www.homesteadhillfarm.com and www.barbarawomack.com

Carlyn Shaw

Carlyn Shaw is an Inspirational Storyteller, Intuitive Connector & Coach and Founder of Strangers To Friends. She empowers people to turn setbacks into stepping stones, let go of limiting labels and say yes to life. In 1998, following an MS diagnosis and the death of best friends, Carlyn began her physical and spiritual awakening. This ignited her self-love journey and intuitive powers. Armed with curiosity, she embraces life as the ultimate experience. Strangers To Friends, a community founded on People = Possibilities, creates opportunities for face to face, authentic connection. Connect with Carlyn at her website www.StrangersToFriends.com and www.CarlynShaw.com IG: @thecarlynshaw

Chelley Canales

Chelley Canales is a budding entrepreneur, writer, speaker and performing artist with a firecracker spirit in a form that can hardly contain it. Founder of lighthouse/haven, a spiritual wellness company. You can read more about Chelley at Chell in the Hallway, a blog about intentionally propelling herself into the unknown, and at chelleycanales.com.

Christine Do

Christine Do is an Earth medicine practitioner who helps others trust in their wisdom of the womb and is on a mission to liberate pleasure and sexuality. She offers her unique gifts and insights and loves creating. Christine enjoys connecting with Gaia and getting her hands dirty in the garden with the flowers and the bees. www.rosetemplearts.com and email at christinedonz@gmail.com

Courtney Beeren

Courtney is an energy healer, psychic medium, writer, and coach. She helps people work through blocks, find direction, understand themselves on a deeper level and take control of their own healing. www.courtneybeeren.com

Dana Lam

Dana is passionate about helping couples to be the Happiest Couples They Know. She is the co-founder of Fun Fantasy Ritual that provides couples coaching and consulting. She wants couples to stay together and it starts with making the romantic relationship a priority. Fun Fantasy Ritual has great resources that can help couples and families. Connect with Dana at: www.FunFantasyRitual.com or info@funfantasyritual.com You can download the free Inspiration Kit and start being the happiest couple you know.

Dana Parker

Dana is a natural born intuitive who only awoke to this when she started to see Spirits after a friend passed away. Now, following a successful corporate management career and dance studio business, Dana offers personal sessions and group events to support others awaken to their innate spiritual gifts. Dana is a certified spiritual advisor (psychic medium) through the Lisa Williams School of International Spiritual development and a Soul (Past) Life Regressionist certified by the Toni Reilly Institute. She specializes in assisting the Divine Sacred feminine rise through her Sacred Sister Soul Circles.
www.danaspiritbutterfly.com / www.sacredroseawakening.com / www.tangobutterfly.com.au

Debra K. Rohrer

Debra K. Rohrer is Owner/Founder of Solutions 4 Life, a Strategic Consulting and Coaching business based in Scottsdale, AZ. She is recognized as a creative, intuitive strategic planner and effective problem solver. Through consultation and coaching, she guides her clients as they reach their vision of what they want to achieve. Debra has over 25 years of experience in strategic consulting and coaching; life transition coaching; addiction recovery coaching; career and educational consulting; entrepreneurial business consulting; corporate consulting and coaching. When not helping people, she loves spending time with her family. Debra earned a

BS in Business from Arizona State University and graduated from Southwest Institute of Healing Arts as a Certified Transformational Life Coach. She is currently completing her MS in Psychology at Grand Canyon University. Debra is available for strategic consulting, coaching and speaking. To connect with her visit www.solutions4lifecoaching.com or contact her at 602-882-0038 and debbie@solutions4lifecoaching.com.

Deedee Panesar

I am an Intuitive Channeler, Visionary Philosopher, Forest Therapist, and world traveler. I live a life that is solitary, open and unrestrained. My mission is to share wisdom and inspiration that enhances your life journey: waking up your inner spirit and expanding your daily happiness. This state of acceptance and presence will aid you in discovering your purpose and co-creating your desires with help from the Universe. The natural state of our soul is love, joy, gratitude, abundance, and creativity. Standing in your true essence you can unleash the power that has been entombed in your soul. DeedeePanesar.com

Dina F. Gilmore

Dina F Gilmore or "She Who Heals Plenty" is a certified Shamanic Practitioner, a Licensed Massage Therapist, Reiki Master Teacher, Photographer, Broadcaster, Podcaster, an author, speaker, and mentor. She grew up in Texas, moved to Colorado in 2012 to thrive in a more diverse state, and build community connections by creating Mobile Shaman to share the ancient art of Shamanism in modern-day society. Dina leads Shamanic Journeys, teaches various healing classes, is currently pursuing her degree in Digital Media Journalism, and is President of Rocky Mountain Media found on Anchor.fm, iTunes, Spotify, and Google Podcasts.
shewhohealsplenty.wixsite.com/mobileshaman
shewhohealsplenty@gmail.com
www.facebook.com/MobileShaman-1223497391116026/
anchor.fm/rocky-mountain-media

Dr. Colleen Brown

Dr. Colleen Brown is an Integrative Veterinarian and Mixed Media Artist in Phoenix, Arizona. She practices Traditional Chinese Veterinary Medicine for dogs, cats, and horses. At times, the healer needs healing and art heals. Her favorite subjects to paint include horses and angels. Dr. Brown lives with her son Tyler, dog Sam, and cats, Sally and Roker. She grew up in Cleveland, Ohio with a very close Irish-Italian family. Her fondest memories include the time spent with her grandparents during her youth. For more information, please go to her website at: brownvetservices.com or email her at soulpuppyhealing@gmail.com.

Dr. Vicki L. High

Dr. Vicki L. High is an acclaimed author, life coach, counselor, speaker, founder of Heart 2 Heart Healing and former mayor. Dr. High, a pioneer in spiritual healing, boldly journeys into new frontiers of freedom, love, empowerment and spiritual insights. She shares wisdom through direct experience in life, intuition, and spiritual realms. Her gifts empower her to connect ideas and concepts and then create patterns for life and healing. She lives through her heart, honoring each person as an aspect of God Source.
Vhigh4444@aol.com
www.heart2heartconnections.us
www.empowereddreams.com
@stoptraumadrama, @kalmingkids, @heart2heartprograms

Gibby Booth Jasper

Hello! Here's where I'm supposed to use the third person and say I live in Massachusetts with my fiancée and dogs. Snore! Instead here's the unboring version: I've always been one to color outside the lines! I love cheese (the sharper the better!), I am terrified of snakes (yes, even the totally harmless ones!), I enjoy house plants but don't have a green thumb at all, and I'm on a mission to reframe the way dyslexia is seen. Visit me: gibbybooth.com or I'd love to hear from you: gibbybooth@gmail.com

Giuliana Melo

Giuliana Melo believes in the Divine healing energy of the Universe. She loves being of service and connecting others to their Divine team of helpers. She is a fun and faithful angel intuitive. Having walked her own journey of cancer and grief, she now supports others through their life struggles with help from God and the angelic realm through angel card readings and angel prayers. If you have been feeling called to get to know your guardian angels or tap into your intuitive gifts, then contact her www.giulianamelo.com

Isaac Bowers

Isaac Bowers, 10 years old, is an avid reader and coder, explorer of nature and lover of video games. He aims to be an evolutionary scientist one day and hopes to publish a solo book of his own. He lives with his family in Dallastown, PA, and hopes others will learn from his experience.

Jaklyn Brockman

Jaki Brockman, born into the Ballroom dancing industry, opened her first studio at age 21. After raising a successful studio for 7 years, Jaki decided to chase her dance dreams and move to New York City! While managing the top Fred Astaire Dance Studio in the nation, she also competed professionally in American Smooth. Winning multiple titles around the US, Jaki decided to move back to Colorado and open Ballroom & Beyond. This past May, Jaki competed at Blackpool Dance Festival in England in Professional American Rhythm. Placing 6th, she is now a finalist in the world's most prestigious competition.

Jeannie Church

Jeannie Church is a Divorce Mediator, Coach, and Healer. Her passion is changing how couples experience divorce by advoc-

ating for resilience and peace during the process. With a Master of Somatic Psychology, she has a holistic approach to compassionately working with the stress and trauma that separation can impose on the mind-body-soul-spirit. Jeannie is also a Reiki Level II Practitioner, a Gong Goddess, and Nature-lover. When she is not mediating you may find her playing with crystals or on a Shamanic Journey somewhere. Contact: 303.903.9226 jeannie.m.church@gmail.com
https://www.truedirectiondivorce.com/
Reference links for Jeannie's article:
http://www.history.com/this-day-in-history/first-divorce-in-the-colonies
https://www.smithsonianmag.com/history/heartbreaking-history-of-divorce-180949439/

Joi Hayes

Joi Hayes is the mother of 3 adult children. She lives in Arizona at the present time. This is Joi's first publication but not won't be her last. Please contact Joi at Cookin4joi@aol.com

Julianna Nelson

Julianna Nelson is passionate about inspiring and supporting individuals and organizations to become social impact leaders in their communities. Her vision is a world where people are working together to accomplish great things! Her nonprofit consulting firm Phillinnova is built on a foundation of compassion, mentorship, and collaboration and the result is thriving, vibrant communities where individuals, businesses and nonprofit organizations are working together for the greater good.
www.phillinnova.com julianna@phillinnova.com 303.552.8780

Katie Hilborn

Katie Hilborn has been at the forefront of empowering women to drive change both locally and abroad since 2006. She's not just speaking about these topics, but she's actually lived them! Her travels to twenty-eight countries and six continents have inspired her to help create positive change by being of service to those living in poverty and struggling in the developing world. In 2011, she founded Global Orphan Prevention and was awarded as the runner-up for Millennial Changemaker of the Year in 2016 for her efforts surrounding the 2015 Nepal earthquake. Her humanitarian work has been featured on the ABC Morning Show, Women of Denver, Impact Founder, Nonprofit Leadership Podcast, and in various media outlets. Currently, she's working on an anti-child trafficking program both in Nepal and Colorado, using microenterprise and awareness campaigns to halt this epidemic. Since 2011, Katie has recruited volunteers and inspired people to help aid her in humanitarian projects totaling over 28,000 hours! www.katiehilborn.com

Karista Rose

Karista Rose is a former foster child born in Kingman, Arizona. She is an inspirational speaker who shares her story of "Defying the Odds." She advocates for causes that have touched her personally, including child abuse, domestic violence, adrenal insufficiency, and chronic pain. She struggles daily with the life-threatening condition of adrenal insufficiency and pain. She touches others' lives through various avenues, including beauty pageants, volunteering and speaking engagements. Karista Rose is the 2018–2019 International Ambassador for Ultimate Elite Pageants. Fun fact: never a dancer, she danced the halftime shows for the both NBA and WNBA. She also has four sphynx cats. Contact: karistarose@yahoo.com, karistarose.com, or Facebook: @KRDefyingtheOdds to follow her mission.

Kat Saraswati

Kat Saraswati is the founder of Serenity Through Sound® which she established with the intent to increase awareness of the therapeutic benefits of harmonics, sound, and vibration and assist others to heal emotional, mental and physical traumas. She is a certified Advanced Level 4 Himalayan Singing Bowl Master, VoiceBio® Sound Therapist, Gong Master, Access Bars®

Practitioner, and Licensed BioGeometry® Environmental Home Solutions Practitioner. Kat integrates BioGeometry® Bio-signatures, balancing techniques and the resonance of gongs and singing bowls to assist her clients in harmonizing their physical, mental and emotional space.

www.SerenityThroughSound.com

717-516-1164 contact@SerenityThroughSound.com

Katie Smock

Katie Smock, Wife, Mom of 5, Entrepreneur with a children's entertainment company and an Adventurer. I love a good story and I like to help others have a good story to tell. That means doing crazy things like picking up your kids in a T-Rex costume or wearing fairy wings to your daughter's softball game. I love to have fun and laugh. My email is:

the6smocks@comcast.net 717-600-9344

Kelsey Quattlebaum

I'm a Holistic Healing Coach, Entrepreneur, and Magic Maker. I blend Shamanic practices, energy work, and bodywork to truly heal my clients from the inside out. By bringing the mind, body, and soul into alignment we take back our personal power. Embodying that higher frequency within ourselves is what enables us to manifest a truly magical reality. I have always found writing to be an immense joy as well as a tool for healing, processing, and so much more. kquattlebaum_94@hotmail.com

Kim Clayton

Kimberly Clayton is a licensed nursing home administrator and former Federal civil servant. She has devoted her life to public service.

Kimber Bowers

Reverend Kimber Bowers is a Mind-Body Wellness speaker and teacher who encourages others to discover and embrace their own power to create and navigate change. It is her purpose to serve as

a reflection of the Love that IS allowing others to discover it within their own lives and souls. Reiki Master, Spiritual Counselor, Clinical Hypnotherapist.
Connect with her at https://www.lovinglighthw.com

Kyra Schaefer

After seeing thousands of clients in her hypnosis practice Kyra decided to shift focus to her true passion. She makes book publishing accessible for aspiring authors at As You Wish Publishing. Kyra creates group books with authors who want to use authorship to help them build their brand in an affordable and easy way all while delivering professionally produced books and media which help readers with personal transformations. www.asyouwishpublishing.com

Leah Recor

Author of "Where the Light Is: A Parent's Guide to the Law of Attraction," Leah Recor is a mother of two young girls. Leah turned personal traumatic experiences into her mission to help other parents. Leah believes in nurturing children's lives psychologically and nutritionally. She introduces easy practices that provide a practical approach to positive parenting. Her online workshops lessen the guilt many parents feel to better connect with their children. Co-Founder of Little Legacies LLC, Leah also mentors children facing serious illness, trauma, and special needs through creative writing.
www.theabundantparent.com @theabundantparent
720-696-1373 theAbundantParent@gmail.com

Leanne Weasner

My journey began thirty-nine years ago. I am a single Mother of a beautiful thirteen-year-old daughter, from the Niagara Region. I spend my days as a Renal Aide in the Kidney Care Program at the SCS Hospital. Pushing through the pain and trials of my journey, I found my passion for writing. Inspiring those on a journey to self-love and healing, my empathy and intuitive mindset allows me to help souls that cross my path in need. I can be reached at lasinspirationalquotes@outlook.com. Visit my facebook page @LAsinspirationalquotes. Love and light to all.

Linda Ingalls

I am a retired ICU RN. Early in my career I learned I was able to speak with my patient's spirits and became known for this ability. Currently, I do Intuitive Counseling, Coaching, Energy Healing, and teach classes to give people the tools to manage their energy so they can have a happier, more loving life. I am happy and grateful to be part of the wonderful team of Practitioners at SpiritQuest Retreats in Sedona, AZ. www.lindaingalls.com

Lucy Sanford

Lucy Sanford's personal journey of transformation is remarkable, having gone from Stage 4 to remission in 3 months, healed a 32-yr auto-immune disease of the thyroid, sleep apnoea and a condition known as Electromagnetic Hyper-Sensitivity. She works with energy as a Geomancer (earth grid lines & geopathic stress), as a certified Electromagnetic Radiation Specialist and as a personal coach, helping people transform their lives by changing their inner and outer environments.
Visit her at www.lucysanford.com.

Marchelle Bentley

Marchelle is a brilliant real-life story teller. She lives in Virginia with her husband and loves animals, the beach and her daughter, Ashley "Kyra" Schaefer.

Mariah Ehlert

I'm Mariah Ehlert, a Neurosculpting® Facilitator, Photographer, and Rebel. I am not a neuroscientist nor a therapist, more of a brain coach, teaching insight into why our brains do what they do, to optimize and improve our daily lives to live with ease, and calm the stress response, and be healthier in mind and body. My approach to healing can often be atypical (rebellious side of me), but that is what worked for me, on my own healing path. I can be found with my two silly border collies at The Rebel Brain, www.therebelbrain.com, me@therebelbrain.com

Marion Andrews

Bestselling author, Marion Andrews strives to impart the knowledge and wisdom she has gained through many classes, certifications, and volunteer leadership positions. Reiki is the way to healing your inner self as well as helping with your physical self. And teaching comes naturally to her. Working with Marion can offer you: Relaxing, restorative Reiki, in person or distant energy work, Meditation, and Online Classes. If you are ready to take a clear look at your life, no holds barred, book some life coaching sessions. Schedule a 15-minute free video call by emailing or messaging Marion at: Mandrews14559@gmail.com www.chrysaliswellnesscenter.com www.facebook.com/ChrysalisWellnessCenter

Michelle Forsyth

Survivor. Fighter. Funny. Dreamer. These are some words that describe Michelle. After years of living with Chronic Fatigue Syndrome, Michelle became an Energy Budget Expert. Michelle worked her way up the corporate ladder, then changed gears and became an entrepreneur and writer. Today, Michelle freelances as a virtual assistant, coach, and of course, a writer. Her self-discovery guided journal, co-written with her mother, Marion Andrews, is available on Amazon and is a wonderful tool to help you discover own rising star qualities by understanding who you are through daily journaling. Learn more about your next journal at https://whoamianywayjournal.com/

Monica Brown

Monica Brown is a Motivational Speaker and Coach. Monica helps high achieving professionals to identify their blind spots so that they can have what they want in their lives. She offers workshops for individuals ready to make changes in their lives,

she works with businesses to improve culture and employee well-being and provides private mentoring.
www.bliss-soul.com. monica@bliss-soul.com. (480) 510-6885.
Www.Facebook.com/MonicaBrownBliss
www.LinkedIn.com/in/Monica-brown-33703022

Nell Jean Mitchell

Retired after forty plus years of teaching with a passion for instructing reading and writing to so many students. Now it's my time to put my own thoughts and experiences on paper. So I have begun! nell24650@cox.net 480 280-5097

Nick Browning

I hold 3 advanced graduate degrees in Psychology and have lived life as much as I can in my short years on this earth. Feel free to reach out to me at nick@auspiciousowl.com or 303.862.6219.

Pedram Owtad

Pedram,has been happily married for over 13 years with a precious 6 year old son. He has always believed in human goodness at the core and knows there is good in everything. Always fascinated with human behavior, spirituality, paradoxically with technology and innovations. Founder of CompuTechNet, a computer company helping thousands of clients for the past 25 years to create peace of mind around technology solutions. He cares for his clients as if they were extended family members. He has been writing and researching for the past 6 years for the book he's planning to publish, titled: "The Secret Cycle of Givers & Receivers", to help to find our purpose in life, by collaborating with each other's unique gifts.

Rachel Gill

Rachel Gill, Lover of photography and a passion for encouraging and uplifting people to be the best version of themselves. A single mom to 6 beautiful kids who spends her time painting, dancing, traveling, and living life outside of the box.

Rosalie Weatherhead

My name is Rosalie Weatherhead. I am an Independent Health-care Advocate. What does that mean? I am the one you turn to when you get no results from your efforts to resolve an issue or communicate with a healthcare professional. I have extensive knowledge and experience in healthcare. But more importantly, I help people. I am not in this to make money or to take advantage. I may die broke but some broke people like me will have a better life because I could help them! You can find me on Facebook at My Healthcare Advocate.

Rosemary Hurwitz MA.PS

Rosemary Hurwitz, a married mom of four young adults, is passionate about an inner-directed life and she found the focus for it in the Enneagram. The Enneagram is a time-honored personality to higher consciousness paradigm used worldwide. She received her Enneagram Certification in an MA. Pastoral Studies program at Loyola University, Chicago, in 2001. Rosemary has studied and taught the Enneagram ever since. She also gives Enneagram-based individual coaching for self-awareness and emotional wellness. Rosemary has a BA in Broadcast Communication, and Certifications in Intuitive Counseling and Angel Card Reading and uses these wisdom traditions in her spiritual teaching and coaching. For over twenty years, Along with her husband she gave Discovery Weekend retreats, patterned after Marriage Encounter, for engaged couples. She is a Professional member of the International Enneagram Association.
Reviews at spiritdrivenliving.com. rosepetalmusic@gmail.com

Sanya Minocha

Sanya Minocha is the founder of Kenshō Wellness. After experiencing chronic pain from a tailbone injury, she has spent the last four years empowering, and truly healing herself. She has developed a holistic approach to achieving health and wellness by treating Body, Mind, and Spirit as one. Feeling inspired to help others restore balance, Sanya formed Kenshō to address a major problem in the world: The disconnection of Body, Mind, and Spirit. Through methods such as Coaching, Ayurveda, and NLP, clients are guided on a journey towards health and wellbeing. Sanya can be contacted through the website www.kenshowellness.com or sanya@kenshowellness.com

Saxon Brazier

Saxon Brazier is a writer, woman's empowerment facilitator, community-minded addictions clinician in training. Her passions lie in helping women overcome great trauma and obstacles having undergone her own in her earlier life. Anything to do with opening the heart and giving the reverence it deserves is where you can find Saxon. www.theheartphilosopher.com

Serissa Asta

serissa.asta@gmail.com

Shamegan Smith

I am a woman who has heart and unconditional love for people. After experiencing and struggling with my own lack of self-love, I want to help people find their purpose by working to inspire and encourage others on how to love themselves unconditionally. Find their voices and become advocates for themselves through God through the process of consecration. I can be contacted at Shameganjsmith@gmail.com (346) 704-9469.

Sherry Hess

Sherry Hess is the creator and founder of Legendary Spice where she offers Flavor with Intention by developing beneficial culinary spice blends. As a published author, she shares her personal journey honoring our sense of taste in her chapter of "Ready To Fly: Stories of Strength and Courage to Inspire Your Journey Forward." Most of all, Sherry is passionate about recognizing how to trust our sense of taste, and the importance of recognizing that Living Flavor is the self-empowering answer to navigating the many faces of "health food" these days.

www.livingflavorrevolution.com
www.legendaryspice.com sherry@legendaryspice.com

Sophia Olivas

Sophia Olivas is the owner of Grey Thorn Marketing, an internet image company with a global portfolio. She founded Hope of Hope, a non-profit focused on alleviating poverty, mental health and violence by working at the root cause and empowering women through technology. She is a United Nations Association Member, an author, and a public speaker. As an adventurer, Sophia has backpacked over 30 countries. She also is a butterfly chaser, tree climber, kite flyer that cart-wheels and walks barefoot on soft grass, has an infectious smile and a wanderlust glow.
Facebook @WhatHopeMeans Twitter @SophiaOlivas
www.hopeofhope.org sophia@hopeofhope.org (480) 382-9237

Stefanie R. Winzer

Stefanie is speaker, writer, coach, and owner of The Art of Breaking Through. After years of allowing stress, guilt, fear, and the expectations of others to rule her life; she was over it. So she began to breakthrough a lifetime of B.S. and learn to truly love herself. Along the way, Stefanie realized she was not alone, there countless others similar struggles. Now through her workshops and individual coaching, Stefanie is helping others create their own breakthrough.
480-382-3341,
theartofbreakingthrough.com
swbreakthrough@gmail.com,
Instagram: @swbreakthrough Facebook: fb.me/swbreakthrough

Tammy Coin

Tammy Coin is an Author, Speaker, Teacher, and Healer. She holds sacred space & helps you locate the unhealed emotions blocking the door to your authentic self. Ms. Coin is the owner of The Doors of Wellness and founded the E.M.I.T., Now! A movement to Empower, Motivate, Inspire and Transform the lives

of others. She is dedicated to making a positive impact in the world by teaching others how to shine.
www.emitnowmovement.com|www.thedoorsofwellness.com
www.tammycoin.com
www.raisingworldchildren.com/author/tammy
www.amazon.com/Tammy-Coin/e/B0768MG3MJ
www.holisticspeakersguild.com/tammy-coin

TC Gavlin

From a young age, TC Gavlin began her journey as a seeker of universal truth and spirituality. She sought Native American teachings and practices, participated in woman's circles, embraced key teachers including Deepak Chopra, Yogi Bhajan, Eckhart Tolle and Dr. Joe Dispenza. She has written journals on daily life and spiritual experiences with the intention of sharing the lessons along the way. She teaches and practices Kundalini Yoga and creates inner peace through daily meditation. She may be reached at tiganine@comcast.net

Tiffany Arenas

I grew up a voracious reader and writer. I loved getting lost in the pages of books and identifying with the characters emotions. I love sharing my favorite children's books with my two-year-old son and Peruvian husband. As I go through a life shift and make big changes, I am writing again to heal and create a new story for myself. I may be reached at ozzy8dove@gmail.com.

Todd Schaefer
Todd and his wife Kyra have helped over 4,000 people in the personal development field while creating a multiple 6-figure business in 3 years. Todd mostly spends his time speaking, writing, publishing, business consulting and life coaching. He is most passionate about applying spiritual principles, psychology and his business experience to help business owners achieve the foundations and build the systems for real-world success. Todd is the author of *The Acceptance Guidebook: Spiritual Solutions for*

Active Minds. He can be contacted for speaking, consulting and coaching via phone or email at his website: http://www.acceptanceguidebook.com/.

Tosha Fields

My name is Tosha and I am a person that tries to view life in many facets and not just by what I see. I try to see the world for the endless possibilities it has. I've been told that I have great patience and I have to believe it's that patience that allows me to see life the way I do. Writing has always been a part of my soul since I was a child. I hope that my story will help at least one person. I can be reached at tosha3510@gmail.com and/or 602-410-0179

Acknowledgments

We want to thank everyone who helped to make this book a success. You have made a difference in our lives. Your love and support has brought us great joy.

Carlos Arenas, Nell Jean-Mitchell, Tom Jean-Mitchell, Malcolm Weatherhead, Sukh Minocha, Lalita Minocha, Rikky Minocha, Sid Menon, Pavan Punjabi, Vala Vincent, Kathy Greiling, Jackie Ganguly, Anibal Canales, Anna Canales, Beverly Saloman, Martin Kupper, Kenya Stewart, Brenda Crimi, Karri Godec, Danell Hunter, Anne Powell, Joe Bowers, Wendy Rodkey, Leigh-Anne MacDonald, Trish Sexton, Kelly Harley, Mia Ferrara, Anne Merrick, Lina Costanzo, Stacey Power, Sarah Ryan, Serenay Kalkan, Jena-Lee Leskie, Arianna Schröder, Yura Viknyansky, Lew Hunter, American Screenwriter/UCLA Chairman Professor Emeritus, Dr. Brenda R. Combs, Tonya Denise Allen, Denise (Bella) Ceballos Viner, Jennifer Knapp, Director, Adrenal Insufficiency United, Catrionna J. Simental, Barrie Tinker, Cristianna G. Borelli, Heather Kirk, Corianna Lee, James Harris, Beverly Saloman, Debra McMichael, Randal, Renee McGee, Autumn Starr, Vicki Vehanen, Joan Wolf, and Lyn Birmingham, Shamegan Smith, Darrian Jackson, Victor Reyes, Dr.Sharon Zygowicz, Eve Higby, Patricia Burrett, Kerri Reynolds, Allyson Wood, Kate Vollmer, Kristy Byfield, Eric Sutfin, Nicole McHenry, Chris Ward, Deb Vera, Loretta De Pellegrin, Cassi Smiley, Nadim Sawaya, Latosha Fields, LaQuincey Valiare, Kendra Brackens, Chante Singleton-Dupree, Marleetha Longs, Kyra Schaefer, Payam Owtad, Shannon Jackson, Heather Macpherson, Janet Holliday, Jaymie Williams, Sandy Gonterman, J'ahmad Kelly, Terry Wilcox, Garrett Hininger, Christen Eve, Lori Coffelt, Susan Bramwell, Susan DuFault, Donna Vogel, Holly

King, Cheri S., Carol H., Marguerite H., Mary S., Tori W., Marian F.,Tina C., Cece M., Danielle Forsyth, Marion Andrews, Annette Gebhardt, Kurt Smock, Miriam Barnes, Carlyn Shaw, Emily Rosen, Kimberley Laurence, Thomasa Semaan, Lora Hulsman, Cary Bailen, Sally, Kellie Springer, Karen Bayless, Sonnie, Corrie Ann Gray, Brittney Drames, Sally Heard, Cherith, Savanna Marie, Sue, Cheryl, Moira, Maria, Emily, Julie, Debbie, Miriam, Dawn, Kiwi, Hunter, Vikki, Nicole, Aranda, Vikki, Nicole, Monica, Elaine, Chris, Kristy, Casey, Krista, Donna, Shannon, Tink,   Noelle, Cindy, Xavier Gill, Denali Gill, Iryna Demyanchuk, Antonia Carey, Nick Palazzo, Kasia Prutis, Dori Wolfe, Alex Lovisetto, Beth Lovisetto, Chip Hickey, Erika Hickey, Bob Rohrer, Marge Rohrer Jazmyn Winzer, Jaida Winzer, Steven Heckroth, Vicki Petosa, Denisha Martin, Jeanne Yancer, Charlie Hatch, RT, Julianna, Annalesa, God, Linda Recors' daughters, Abraham-Hicks, Shanda Trofe, Todd Schaefer, Honey, Jack, Laura Rudacille, Julia Smith Reda, Patty Glorioso, Karen Brisson, Odette Karlsson, Natalie Kipling, Ciara Bowers, Cooper Bowers, Emil Reda, Tiffany Arenas, Margaret Hvizda, Katie Brown, Santa Loparo, Heather Dunning, Grace Dunning, Holly Alexander, Grace Kirtner, Jenny Kraakevik, Robert Parker, and Leonie Parker.

Thank you for reading *When I Rise, I Thrive*

We would love to hear about your story. You can contact us at Kyra@asyouwishpublishing.com

As You Wish Publishing

Giving Voice to Your Story

Join our next project, create your own group project or individual book by visiting us here at www.asyouwishpublishing.com to learn more.

Collaborative books published by As You Wish Publishing

Happy Thoughts Playbook

When I Rise, I Thrive

Healer

Made in the USA
Middletown, DE
05 February 2019